THE
Rock 'n' Pop
QUIZ
BOOK

THE
Rock 'n' Pop
QUIZ
BOOK

Eric Saunders

ARCTURUS

ARCTURUS

This edition published in 2009 by Arcturus Publishing Limited
26/27 Bickels Yard, 151–153 Bermondsey Street,
London SE1 3HA

ISBN: 978-1-84837-222-1
AD000391EN

Printed in Singapore

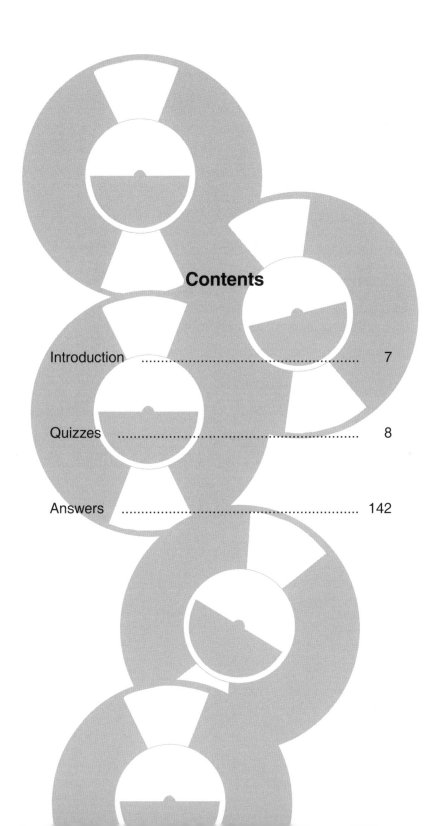

Contents

The Rock 'n' Pop Quiz Book is a celebration of the rich variety of entertainment brought to us by the music industry. Each successive generation has spawned its own pop/rock culture and so this book has been created to span virtually all eras and genres of rock and pop music, from the late 1940s to the present day, with questions for young and old alike. Some questions are hard and some are easy but I hope all are interesting and entertaining.

Don't worry if you find that some artists, bands, etc, are unfamiliar; you can't know them all! Maybe certain new names might just intrigue your curiosity into discovering new sounds and styles.

So sit back with family and friends and find out just how well you know your music!

Eric Saunders

1 What was Fats Domino's real first name?

2 Which black American group took their name from the US slang term for gramophone records?

3 In 1960, which American rock 'n' roll legend died, aged just 21, in a freak automobile accident at Chippenham, England?

4 Having survived a serious motorcycle accident five years earlier, which other great singer again cheated death in the accident referred to in Question 3?

5 What was the name of the weird act that had a scorching hit with *Fire* in 1968?

6 *Bleeding Love* was a No 1 hit single in 2008. Who was the solo female singer of this song?

7 Which record producer is famous for his 'wall of sound' technique?

8 Whitney Houston's massive hit *I Will Always Love You* was featured in which movie of 1992?

9 Which band featured in Mariah Carey's 1995 hit *One Sweet Day*?

10 Whose songs include the hits *Galveston* and *Wichita Lineman*?

11 In 2004, who finally released the album *Smile* after a thirty-plus year wait?

12 What was the title of the Pussycat Dolls No 1 single which peaked in June 2005?

13 Which British band has notched up over a hundred million album sales in the USA, with one of their biggest hit singles being *Whole Lotta Love* from 1969?

14 Which heavy metal band's albums include *And Justice For All* and *Master Of Puppets*?

15 Which American crooner made several comedy films with Jerry Lewis?

16 In 2008, which late rock band member overtook Elvis Presley as the world's top deceased money-earner?

1 Which early rock 'n' roll artiste (born 1908) was nicknamed 'King of the Jukebox'?

2 Originally recorded by Big Joe Turner in 1954, which song was made more famous by Bill Haley's version of the same year?

3 Which famous recording studio stands at 706 Union Avenue, Memphis, Tennessee?

4 "I know a girl from a lonely street, cold as ice-cream but still as sweet" are lyrics from which song from a band which hit the music scene in the late 1970s?

5 Dave Grohl left Nirvana to form which band in 1994?

6 How is Gordon Matthew Thomas Sumner better known to the world at large?

7 At which New York stadium did the Beatles perform during their record-breaking tour of America in August 1965?

8 What was the name of Martha Reeves' backing group?

9 Performed by the Righteous Brothers, *Unchained Melody* was used in which movie of 1986?

10 What was the highly unusual cause of the death, on Christmas Day 1954, of R&B singer Johnny Ace?

11 Starring Jamie Foxx in the title role, which movie of 2004 portrays the career of a famous American soul singer?

12 *Climb Every Mountain* and *Edelweiss* are two of the many songs from which 1965 movie?

13 Who was popularly known as 'The First Lady of Song'?

14 Which British female singer had a string of hits in America in the 1960s including *Son Of A Preacher Man* and *You Don't Have To Say You Love Me*?

15 What nationality is singer/songwriter and actress Natalie Imbruglia?

16 Which pop/country music singer released his album *The Lost Sessions* in 2005?

1. What do the 'k' and the 'd' stand for in k.d. lang's name?

2. Which Turkish-born record producer founded Atlantic Records in the late 1940s?

3. In 1947, Jerry Wexler was reputed to have coined the term 'Rhythm and Blues'. For which music journal was he writing at the time?

4. Wild Bill Moore, who released *We're Gonna Rock, We're Gonna Roll* in 1948, was a master of which instrument?

5. For what main reason did Bob Dylan receive a great deal of criticism from certain quarters over his 1965 album *Bringing It All Back Home*?

6. Kylie Minogue's *Loco-Motion* of 1988 was originally a big hit for which singer in 1962?

7. *Grief Never Grows Old,* a single recorded by an ad hoc band which included Brian Wilson and Barry and Robin Gibb, was released in aid of the victims of which 2004 catastrophe?

8. The Eagles originally formed as the backing group for which female singer?

9 Which American girl-band was originally called '2nd Nature'?

10 Which famous singer has appeared in the movies *The Fresh Prince Of Bel Air, The Jerky Boys, Mars Attacks!* and *Agnes Browne*?

11 After which Vulcan character out of TV's *Star Trek* was a certain 1980s band named?

12 Quentin Crisp, the English writer, was the inspiration for which song by Sting?

13 *Lovefool* by the Cardigans featured in which movie starring Leonardo DiCaprio?

14 Which 'Man in Black' was once a 'Boy Named Sue'?

15 Which singer, known internationally by her first name only, has the surname of Gudmundsdottir?

16 Which is the best-selling of Simon & Garfunkel's albums?

1. *Walking In the Rain* and *Such A Night* were hits for which Oregon-born singer who had considerable influence on rock 'n' roll in its early days?

2. At the same time as carving out his own very successful career as a singer, who wrote the Monkees songs *I'm a Believer* and *A Little Bit Me, A Little Bit You*?

3. *OG: Original Gangster* was a 1991 album for which rap singer?

4. Established classic rock 'n' roll is usually played using which combination of instruments?

5. Don McLean's song which starts with the words "Starry starry night" was a tribute to which famous artist?

6. The 1963 single *Come On* was the very first release of which major band who are still active in 2008?

7. Which great female country music singer died in a plane crash on March 5th 1963?

8. The pop and folk band The Corrs come from which country?

9 The Sex Pistols and The Clash were early exponents of which genre of popular music?

10 Which famous rock album has on its front cover an underwater shot of a baby swimming towards a dollar bill?

11 *American Gothic* was a 2008 album released by which alternative rock band?

12 Which band was originally named Angel and the Snakes?

13 Which singer is the daughter of one of the founding members of the Simon & Schuster publishing house?

14 Real name Richard Hall, which singer's stage name is derived from the title of a famous novel whose author happens to be an ancestor of the singer?

15 First formed in the early 1960s, which rock band still continues to perform with two of its original members Pete Townshend and Roger Daltrey?

16 Whose 2005 album was entitled *Confessions on a Dance Floor*?

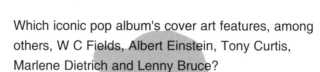

1 Which iconic pop album's cover art features, among others, W C Fields, Albert Einstein, Tony Curtis, Marlene Dietrich and Lenny Bruce?

2 What was the name of Bill Haley's backing group before they were renamed to the Comets in the early 1950s?

3 Which singer hosted her tenth consecutive Academy of Country Music Awards in 2008?

4 *Nothing But The Best* was a 2008 retrospective album of the songs by which singer?

5 What was Bruce Springsteen's Academy Award-winning movie song of 1993?

6 Who released her *Songs In A Minor* album in 2001?

7 Which rock 'n' roll/blues singer had the nickname 'The Originator'?

8 Who had a 1966 No 1 hit in America and many other countries with the novelty song *These Boots Are Made For Walkin'*?

9 Directed by Wim Wenders, which 1999 documentary movie is about the music of Cuba?

10 Which Cleveland-based DJ is often credited with coining the term 'rock and roll' in around 1951?

11 Which songstress co-produced the single *Impossible* with Christina Aguilera?

12 Which band had great success with their *Rumours* album?

13 Which band's name was taken from a magazine headline telling of Frank Sinatra's move from Las Vegas to Hollywood?

14 Bob Dylan's *All Along The Watchtower* was covered by which rock legend in the late 1960s?

15 Which drummer, who released *Drum Rolls And Samples,* joined Aerosmith at the age of 18 years?

16 Who had big hits with *Big Yellow Taxi* and *Woodstock*?

1   In 1962, which British jazz musician had a big hit on both sides of the Atlantic with *Stranger on the Shore,* a title covered by Andy Williams in the same year?

2   Which 2001 album by Robbie Williams was inspired by the songs and style of Frank Sinatra?

3   Which hip-hop/reggae star burnt his fingers when he set fire to his guitar at 'Woodstock 1999'?

4   Which rock star married Lisa Marie Presley in 1994?

5   What was the stage name of the rock 'n' roll and blues singer who was born Ellas Otha Bates?

6   In 2005, who released an album entitled *Devils and Dust*?

7   The singer Björk, who has had less success in America than in the rest of the world, comes originally from which country?

8   In 1967, which Beatles song reached No 1 in America but was the first not to reach No 1 in the UK since 1963?

9   Which highly successful US band's collaboration broke up with a fight after a concert at Long Beach, California in July 1980?

10   Who started his music career as 'The Hillbilly Cat'?

11   What is the better-known name of Tracy Marrow?

12   Quentin Tarantino's film *Pulp Fiction* featured which well-known Dusty Springfield song?

13   Bill Haley's *Rock Around The Clock* was used in which gritty movie of 1955?

14   In 1999, which female artist had a No 1 hit single with *Genie In A Bottle*?

15   Which movie actress/singer had a 1999 No 1 hit single with *If You Had My Love*?

16   Which American band had hits in the 1960s with songs such as *Proud Mary* and *Bad Moon Rising*?

1   In which year was the Elvis Presley movie *Jailhouse Rock* released?

2   *Lest We Forget: The Best Of* was the 2004 compilation album of which notorious singer/band?

3   Which INXS singer was found dead in a Sydney hotel room in 1997?

4   Which rock icon released his second *Crossroads Guitar Festival* in 2007?

5   When Buddy Holly was tragically killed in an airplane crash in 1959, which two fellow stars died with him?

6   American record label CBS was bought out by which corporation in 1988?

7   Which black American singer is remembered for her renditions of *God Bless The Child* and *Gloomy Sunday*?

8   How is Cherilyn Sarkisian La Pierre better known to the world?

9 Which British singer was signed up by the American S-Curve label and produced her first album *The Soul Sessions* in 2003?

10 What was the title of the Annie Lennox 2007 album which made No 9 in the American charts?

11 The 2004 movie *Beyond The Sea,* starring Kevin Spacey, was about which American singer?

12 In the 1950s, rock 'n' roll quickly rippled across the Atlantic and found a ready audience in the UK. Which British singer had a hit with *Move It* in 1958?

13 Which singer's first American No 1 single was *Fingertips – Part 2* (1963) and his last *That's What Friends Are For* (1985)?

14 Which band's song *Dancing Queen* was their only one to have made a Billboard Hot 100 No 1?

15 Beyoncé was the first lead singer with which girl-band?

16 Whose best-selling album is the 1984 *Purple Rain*?

1 In 1956, which singer advised, in energetic fashion, Ludwig van Beethoven to 'roll over'?

2 Neil Diamond starred in which 1980 movie – a remake of an Al Jolson classic?

3 The heads of the members of which rock band replaced those of American presidents at Mt Rushmore on the cover of a famous album of 1970?

4 Which singer is the daughter of the sitarist Ravi Shankar?

5 Which band had an American No 1 hit with their 2005 album *X&Y*?

6 In 1962, B Bumble and the Stingers released their famous instrumental number *Nut Rocker*. On whose classical ballet music was this based?

7 Paul McCartney married which American in March 1969?

8 Which band from Gary, Indiana was comprised at various times by brothers Jackie, Tito, Jermaine, Marlon, Michael and Randy?

9 Which singer from The Monkees started his showbiz career on the 1950s TV series *Circus Boy*?

10 Which American singer released her 'best of' album *Retrospective* in 2003?

11 Who starred and sang the title song in the movie *Nine to Five*?

12 James Jewel Osterberg is better known by his stage name. What is it?

13 "Load up on guns, bring your friends, it's fun to lose..." are the opening lyrics from which famous song?

14 Which Frank Sinatra song was karaoke fan Romy Baligula performing when, in 2007, he was shot dead in a Filipino bar for singing out of tune?

15 *Hymns Of The 49th Parallel* was a 2004 album by which Canadian singer?

16 Which Elvis Presley movie had the original title *The Reno Brothers*?

QUIZ 9

1 Released in 1955 as a single, which song by Chuck Berry told of a hot rod race and a failed love affair?

2 Whose album *The Division Bell* stayed at No 1 for four weeks in 1994?

3 Which American hard rock band are known as 'The Bad Boys from Boston'?

4 In 1980, which rock band broke up after the death of its drummer John Bonham?

5 Which American hard rock band is comprised of three members with the same surname, plus David Lee Roth?

6 What was the title of the 2003 Lou Reed album inspired by the writings of Edgar Allan Poe?

7 Which of Elvis Presley's songs has the lines "Well it took my baby, but it never will again"?

8 What was the title of the Mason Williams' instrumental hit of 1968?

9 *That Don't Impress Me Much, You've Got A Way* and *From This Moment On* are all tracks that appear on which album of 2000?

10 What was the major track on The Verve's 1997 album *Urban Hymns* which caused a big copyright problem?

11 Which clean-cut singer from the 1950s recorded cooled-down versions of Little Richards' *Long Tall Sally* and *Tutti Frutti*?

12 Which all-female band's 2006 'Accidents and Accusations' tour took them not only across North America but Europe and Australia as well?

13 A very early rock 'n' roll record, *Rocket 88*, by Jackie Brenston and the Delta Cats, was written by which musician, the one-time husband of an iconic black female singer?

14 Which singer is famous for his hits *Me And Bobby McGee* and *Help Me Make It Through the Night*?

15 Which band released the album *9.0 Live* in 2005?

16 Which band lost Hillel Slovak when he died in 1988?

1   The Rock and Roll Hall of Fame and Museum stands on the shore of which of the Great Lakes?

2   Which band wrote the 'rock opera' *Tommy*?

3   Which Bob Dylan song's first words are "Mama take this badge off of me"?

4   Which Michael Jackson song's first words are "What about sunrise, what about rain"?

5   Lisa Lopes of TLC was killed in an automobile accident in 2002. In which country did this happen?

6   Which Beatles song is reputed to be the most covered song in musical history?

7   Whose self-financed live show was recorded onto LP in 1963 under the title *Live At The Apollo*?

8   Whose albums *Pearl*, *In Concert* and *Super Hits* were released posthumously?

9 Which black American singer is famous for her renditions of *What A Difference A Day Makes* and *Mad About The Boy*?

10 *The Night They Drove Old Dixie Down* was the biggest American success for which singer?

11 Gerry Garcia was the lead man with which rock band?

12 The singer Katie Melua was born in which ex-Soviet country?

13 Who starred as the female lead in the Elvis Presley movie *Viva Las Vegas*?

14 Which pop legend was born Reginald Dwight?

15 Who teamed up with Nancy Sinatra in the song *Did You Ever*?

16 Whose album *Growing Pains* was released in 2007?

1 Vocal group The Famous Flames most famously accompanied which singer during the 1950s and early 1960s?

2 Which Michigan-born punk rocker is alleged to have avoided the draft by pretending to be gay?

3 Although the song was unfinished at his untimely death in 1980, who recorded *Free as a Bird* on a tape machine in his New York apartment?

4 Which British-born singer/actress' TV show brought *The Simpsons* to fame in the 1980s?

5 Who had big hits with songs such as *Twenty-Four Hours From Tulsa* and *I'm Gonna Be Strong*?

6 Which pop band (their name contains a number, four) has had over thirty different personnel during the forty-plus years since the band's incorporation?

7 Which singer/songwriter/instrumentalist has the nickname 'The Killer'?

8 Which zany singer, who came to prominence in the 1960s, had the real name of Herbert Khaury?

9 What do Nelson Eddy, Johnny 'Guitar' Watson and Judge Dread have in common?

10 The documentary movie *No Direction Home*, directed by Martin Scorsese, concerns the life and work of which musician?

11 The Tennessee Three was for more than 40 years the backing group for which great singer?

12 'Hitsville USA', the adopted name of a building located on West Grand Boulevard, Detroit, served as the HQ for which record company in the 1950s and 1960s?

13 Which dance, popular during World War II, and named after a condition suffered by alcoholics, was a precursor of rock 'n' roll?

14 *Jazz On A Summer's Day*, a documentary movie filmed in 1958 and featuring, among others, Chuck Berry, was made at which jazz festival?

15 Which American city features in the title of a song, originally by Kirsty MacColl in 1987, that was covered by The Pogues and several others?

16 The Doors rock band was fronted by which iconic lead vocalist?

1   What is Little Richard's actual name?

2   Which children's story inspired the name of Michael Jackson's California ranch?

3   Which singer appeared in the movies *Catch 22* and *Carnal Knowledge*?

4   The 2002 movie *8 Mile* starred which rap singer?

5   Who shot to international fame after her first album *Baby One More Time* was released in 1999?

6   Which American punk rock band was founded by Joey, Johnny and Dee Dee, all of whom shared the same stage 'family' name despite being unrelated?

7   R&B legend Ray Charles used only his first and middle names during his stage career. What was his family name?

8   For which music magazine's 1000th edition, in 2006, was the front cover artwork inspired by that of the Beatles' *Sgt Pepper's Lonely Hearts Club Band* album?

9 In 1995, *Made in Heaven* was the last studio album to be released by which band?

10 Whose songs *Bird On A Wire*, *Chelsea Hotel* and *Halleluja* appear, amongst others, on his 'best of' album released in 2002?

11 *Rock The Joint* was a very early (1949) rock 'n' roll hit for which singer and his band?

12 Which singer married movie director Guy Ritchie in 2000?

13 Which band's album *Dr Feelgood* made No 1 in 1989?

14 Which band took its name from unexplained aerial phenomena seen by flight crews during World War II?

15 *Beautiful Brother: The Essential __* is part of the title of which artist's compilation album, released in 2000?

16 Also known as Doctor Feelgood in his later career, how was Wiliam Lee Perryman better known during the 1940s/50s?

1 What is country singer LeAnn Rimes's first name?

2 *Why Do Fools Fall In Love,* later covered by the Beach Boys and others, was a hit song originally recorded in 1956 by which group?

3 Which world-renowned rock band is fronted by singer, Bono?

4 *Eve Of Destruction* was the title of a 1965 No 1 protest song by which singer?

5 By what name were the Supremes previously known?

6 The Fugees had great international success with *Killing Me Softly* in 1996. Who first made the song famous in 1973?

7 Who, in 1956, was signed up as Elvis Presley's manager?

8 Built on the site of the Stax Records studio, in which American city would you find the Stax Museum, opened in 2003?

9 Which alternative rock band's album *Ta Dah* achieved American chart success in 2006?

10 Which Canadian singer won Best Jazz Vocal Grammy awards in 1999 and 2002?

11 At the US *Superbowl 35* in 2001, along with Nelly and Britney Spears, which solo star appeared with Aerosmith and N'Sync?

12 On whose show did Gene Vincent make his first national TV appearance in 1956?

13 What item of American communications technology was the subject of the title of British group The Tornados No 1 hit instrumental single of 1962?

14 *My Love* and *What Goes Around Comes Around* were No 1 hit singles by which singer?

15 Which songwriting duo penned the hits *Pleasant Valley Sunday* and *Will You Still Love Me Tomorrow*?

16 In an era when new dance crazes came and went almost weekly, which 1960 'invention' stayed a little longer than all the others of that year?

1 Which record executive founded Asylum Records in 1970 and went on to also become a movie and theater director?

2 *Under the Boardwalk* was a big hit in 1964 for which group?

3 Which year: The Everly Brothers make their first recording; sales of 45rpm overtake 78s for the first time; Elvis Presley signs with RCA?

4 *Love To Love You Baby* was the first No 1 single for which singer?

5 In 2000, which band released the album *Chocolate Starfish And The Hot Dog Flavored Water*?

6 In 2005, who released *On Ne Change Pas,* a compilation album sung solely in her original language?

7 *All Things Must Pass* is an album released by which ex-Beatle shortly after the band broke up?

8 In which year was Elvis Presley drafted into the US Army?

9 Dubbed the 'Queen of Latin Pop', which singer, then aged one year, fled with her parents from Cuba in 1959?

10 Which former lead singer with The Commodores started his solo career in 1982?

11 Which British band had great success in America during the 1960s/70s with, among other albums, *Days Of Future Passed* and *A Question Of Balance*?

12 *Running Scared* was the first No 1 hit for which singer in 1961?

13 The 1971 movie *Shaft* had a great title song; it was performed by which singer?

14 Celine Dion sang *My Heart Will Go On* for which blockbuster movie of 1997?

15 Still active in 2007, the band Kraftwerk, founded in 1970, hails from which country?

16 In 1958, which American singer had almost all his British concerts canceled when it was discovered that his wife was only 13 years old?

1 For what reason did Little Richard temporarily retire from the music business in 1958?

2 Movie-wise, what do Tom Jones, Nancy Sinatra, Matt Monro, Carly Simon, Sheena Easton and Tina Turner all have in common?

3 Texas-born Robert Matthew van Winkle is better known by what stage name?

4 *I Knew You Were Waiting (For Me)* was a No 1 hit for which duet back in 1987?

5 Which record label was founded by Berry Gordy in 1958?

6 *It's Raining Men* is possibly the best-known single by which girl band?

7 Under what collective name did forty-plus singers, including Michael Jackson and Bruce Springsteen, record *We Are The World* in 1985?

8 Who won the 2008 Grammy Song of the Year Award for her song *Rehab*?

9   How old was Brenda Lee when she signed a recording contract in 1956?

10   Who won the 2005 Grammy Song of the Year Award for his song *Daughters*?

11   Which disco-dance band had successes with songs such as *YMCA* and *In The Navy*?

12   Who is the youngest performer of the famous Jackson (from Gary, Indiana) family of singers?

13   The classics *Summertime Blues* and *C'mon Everybody* were originally recorded by which singer?

14   Who recorded the Christmas classic *When A Child Is Born*?

15   *Wooden Heart*, an Elvis Presley song which featured in his movie *G I Blues*, was based on a folk song from which country?

16   What was the 1931 invention of Adolph Rickenbacker which helped rock 'n' roll and virtually every other music genre from the 1950s onwards?

1 To which long-running TV series was *Suicide Is Painless* the catchy theme tune?

2 Which 1977 album by Meatloaf has notched up worldwide sales of over 37 million?

3 *Don't Worry, Be Happy* was a No 1 hit and Grammy Award winner in 1988/89 for which singer?

4 *No Woman No Cry* was one of the biggest successes for which reggae act?

5 Whose first No 1 album was *Billion Dollar Babies* in 1973?

6 Who had hits in the 1960s with *Walk On By* and *Do You Know The Way To San José*?

7 Which rock band released their fourteenth album, *Accelerate*, in 2008?

8 The theme song for the *James Bond* movie *A View To A Kill* was performed by which band?

9 Which famous American bomber airplane was the subject of a single by Orchestral Manoeuvres in the Dark, and also covered by several bands since its release in 1980?

10 What was the 1991 hit by TV's *The Simpsons*?

11 Which rap singer is a former member of R&B band Sista, where she was known as 'Misdemeanor'?

12 What was the name of the band associated with Kenny Rogers when their hit *Ruby, Don't Take Your Love To Town* was released in 1969?

13 The singer Shakira, whose album *Laundry Service* achieved great worldwide success, was born in which country?

14 Which band took off on their Voodoo Lounge World Tour in 1994?

15 *Ain't No Mountain High Enough* was the first No 1 single for which singer in 1970?

16 *Got To Be There* was the first solo studio album for which singer?

1   Which singer's album *Play* was his first to achieve worldwide acclaim?

2   *Up Where We Belong* was a No 1 hit for Jennifer Warnes and Joe Cocker in 1982. In which movie of that year did the song feature?

3   Which heavy-metal rocker is reputed to have bitten off the head off a bat during a concert in 1982?

4   Which band's successful albums include *Travelling Without Moving* and *Synkronized*?

5   Which hip-hop star died in a drive-by shooting in Las Vegas in September 1996?

6   "A winter's day, in a deep and dark December" are the opening lyrics to which Paul Simon song?

7   Who started his singing career with the R&B band New Edition and later started a solo act which resulted in his first major success, the album *Don't Be Cruel*?

8   What was the evocative stage name of Lecil Travis Martin (1931-99), a country and gospel singer/ songwriter?

9 Whose record, *Here Come The Judge* (1968), was possibly the earliest example of the genre of rap music?

10 *Tuesday Night Music Club* was the 1993 debut album of which singer?

11 Which American city is associated with the origins of grunge music, which emerged there in the 1980s?

12 In which year were Elvis and Priscilla Presley divorced?

13 Which famous drummer died from a drugs overdose on September 7th 1978?

14 Which 1960s group comprised John and Michelle Phillips, Cass Elliot and Denny Doherty?

15 In which country, in 1991, did Ray Charles have a brush with police after a drugs sniffer dog pounced on him, only for the police to find that Charles had a pack of pork rind snacks in his pocket?

16 *Everybody's Talkin'* earned Harry Nilsson a Grammy Award for Best Male Pop Vocal Performance. In which movie did the song appear?

1   Which rock icon has been credited with the forming of the E Street Band in 1972?

2   Which star of country, folk and rock music studied literature at Oxford University in England during the 1950s?

3   An electronic gadget based on the weird-sounding theremin instrument is featured In which Beach Boys No 1 single of 1966?

4   Who committed *Murder On The Dancefloor*, a hit single from 2001?

5   Who was responsible for *Good Girl Gone Bad*, a hit album from 2007?

6   Which singer/songwriter had former associations with The Range and The Noisemakers?

7   Which rock star played the part of Eddie in *The Rocky Horror Picture Show*?

8   Who launched her solo career with the album *Koo Koo* in 1981?

9. In which Alabama town was Jackson Highway studios, scene of many famous recordings, which closed down in 2005?

10. In 2003, which band embarked on their *Riot Act* tour in support of their album of the same name?

11. What was the famous invention of a certain Mrs Nesmith, mother of Mike Nesmith of the Monkees?

12. Which 1979 single by The Beach Boys contained the melody to a famous piece written by J S Bach in 1723?

13. Which mind-training technique was introduced by the guru Maharishi Mahesh Yogi to the Beatles and others in the 1960s?

14. *Back On The Chain Gang*, from their album *Learning To Crawl*, was a big success for which 'New Wave' genre Anglo-American band?

15. Which thrash metal band broke up in 2002 after its frontman, Dave Mustaine, suffered a severe arm injury? The band re-formed in 2004.

16. Which famous song by The Kinks was inspired by an encounter with a transvestite?

1 Which band took its name from a 1960s hairstyle which, in turn, is taken from the shape of a certain American bomber-plane's nose-cone?

2 Whose only No 1 single was *Make It With You*?

3 *That's The Way Of The World* was a 1970s movie which featured which R&B band?

4 His home town of Baltimore named August 19th as 'his day'; to which rock musician (1940-93) is the day dedicated?

5 Brothers Jordan and Jonathan Knight were two of the line-up for which very successful 1980s/90s boy band?

6 Which band were catapulted to fame with their single *Born to be Wild*, especially after it was used in the movie *Easy Rider*?

7 Which member of The Supremes died suddenly and unexpectedly in February of 1976?

8 What was the title of Tina Turner's breakthrough album of 1984, which featured her classic song *What's Love Got To Do With It*?

9 The *Billboard Hot 100* was launched in which year of the 1950s?

10 Which Los Angeles band changed its name from The Bangs after being threatened with a law suit by a New Jersey band of the same name?

11 The novels *Soft Machine* and *Nova Express* by William S Burroughs are often cited as being the origins of the name of which genre of rock music?

12 *Wonder Boys,* a 2000 movie starring Michael Douglas, featured which song by Bob Dylan?

13 *Love Song For A Vampire* was the closing theme song from the movie *Bram Stoker's Dracula.* By whom was the song performed?

14 What was Chuck Berry's big hit with which he made something of a comeback in 1972?

15 What was the title of the song performed by LeAnn Rimes and Ronan Keating and released in 2004?

16 In 1968, which band was formed by ex-members of The Byrds, The Hollies and Buffalo Springfield?

1   From whose song *Jean Genie* did the band Simple Minds get its name?

2   Which singer played the part of Cleo Hewitt in the 1980s TV series *Fame*?

3   Which famous disco song by Gloria Gaynor has been covered by Gladys Knight and The Pips, Diana Ross and the Crazy Frog?

4   In 1969, which band's first No 1 single was *I Want You Back*?

5   Which Bob Dylan song was a big hit for The Byrds in 1965?

6   In which American city would you find a commemorative statue of singer Hank Williams?

7   Which British band was performing in Cincinnati on December 3rd 1979 when eleven people were crushed to death in a panic to get into the concert?

8   Which classic song was performed by Tina Turner with Rod Stewart in 1990?

9 Who had a hit in 1990 with *Tom's Diner*?

10 Which singer's chart successes include the albums *Are You Gonna Go My Way* and *Circus*?

11 Who was dubbed 'The High Priestess of Soul'?

12 Whose album *Sketches For My Sweetheart The Drunk* was left unfinished at the time of his tragic death in a swimming accident in 1997?

13 Which album by The Beach Boys was inspired by The Beatles' album *Rubber Soul* ?

14 *Viva La Vida, Or Death And All His Friends* was the fourth studio album to be released by which band in 2008?

15 Featuring the hit single *Mr Jones*, which band released its debut album *August And Everything After* in 1994?

16 Which American singer, who died in 1996 aged 33, recorded classic versions of *Over The Rainbow, Fields of Gold* and covers of many other standards? Three of her albums, all posthumous releases, made No 1 in the UK.

1 On first joining the band in 1970, who was Aerosmith's drummer?

2 Frances Bean Cobain is the daughter of Kurt Cobain and which star?

3 The *Logical Song* and *Take The Long Way Home* were the two US best-selling albums of which band?

4 *Just Because I'm A Woman* was the first hit single for which country singer?

5 *Kid A, Amnesiac* and *Hail To The Thief* were all hit albums in the 2000s for which band?

6 *Behind The Bridge To Elephunk* was the title of a 2004 video by which American hip hop and rap band?

7 *Runaway* was the first No 1 hit, in 1961, for which singer?

8 *If You Tolerate This Your Children Will Be Next* was a minor American hit in 1998 for which British band?

9 Robbie Williams and Nicole Kidman duetted on which song in 2001? It was originally recorded by an American father and offspring duo in 1967.

10 Which 2000 Britney Spears album broke records for being the fastest-selling album up until that time?

11 What does WOMAD stand for – the name of the music festivals which have taken place in several parts of the world since 1982?

12 Probably best remembered for their single *Bang A Gong* which band were named after a dinosaur?

13 Which Canadian-born singer's album *Shine* made the American charts in 2007?

14 Which singer had American Top Ten successes with singles including *The Night Has A Thousand Eyes* and *Take Good Care Of My Baby*?

15 The Flying Burrito Brothers were formed by members of which earlier band?

16 The Waitresses provided the theme song for which TV comedy series starring Sarah Jessica Parker?

1 Ben E King left which R&B group to start a solo career in 1960?

2 Whose *James Bond Theme*, from his album *I Like To Score*, scored a hit single in 1997?

3 Which rock band is sometimes called QOTSA?

4 Which iconic instrumental by the Surfaris (with its famous manic gleeful laughter at the beginning) still remains popular forty-plus years after its release?

5 Why did 200,000 people go to Yasgur's farm in 1969?

6 What was the name of the travelling, female artist-only, music festival which ran from 1997 to 1999 across 40 venues in North America?

7 What was the title of Big Star's debut album, which unfortunately, in spite of its good critical reception, didn't live up to its name?

8 Which band's successful albums include *Brothers in Arms* and *On Every Street*?

9   In 2001, which American group covered *Emotion*, a Bee Gees-written song released originally by Samantha Sang?

10   Madonna sang which famous Don McLean song for the 2000 movie *The Next Best Thing*?

11   Which album by Santana went 15 times platinum in America in 1999?

12   Which Beatles album cover shows the band walking in line over a crosswalk?

13   Which Pink Floyd album cover shows a refracting prism against a black background?

14   With sales of over 100 million units, which is the best-selling album of all time?

15   Who sang the national anthems of both the United States and Canada at a 2007 Stanley Cup Finals game between the Anaheim Ducks and Ottawa Senators?

16   What is the family name of brothers Angus and Malcolm who formed the band AC/DC in Australia in 1973?

1 Performed by Cass Dillon, *Christmas In Fallujah*, released in 2007, was written by which musician?

2 The title of which 2003 Linkin Park album was inspired by a mountain monastery in Greece?

3 Which of the Spice Girls married soccer player David Beckham in 1999?

4 Which 1958 release by The Champs has been used in the movie *Pee-Wee's Big Adventure* and in several TV series? The only word sung is the title (three times).

5 Which singer, of Puerto Rican descent, was born Enrique Martin Morales?

6 Which country singer, who retired in 2001, has sold over 100 million records in the US?

7 *Funny Girl* and *Yentl* are just two of the many movies starring which popular singer?

8 Whose 1996-97 *Wildest Dreams* tour took her to five continents in 15 months?

9 On the album *Bridge Over Troubled Water,* to which architect do Simon & Garfunkel say "so long"?

10 The albums *Black Cherry* and *Supernature* provided three No 1 singles for which band?

11 Which rap duo made their recording debut in 1994 with *Southernplayalisticadillacmuzik*?

12 *What A Wonderful World,* covered by dozens of artists, was originally a major success for which musician in 1967?

13 Kirk Jones is the rather more prosaic real name of which rap artist?

14 Michael Jackson's *Bad* video was directed by which American movie director?

15 *Landslide* by the Dixie Chicks, a big hit in 2002, was originally released by which band in 1998?

16 *Blue Monday* was recorded by Fats Domino in 1956 and by which band in 1983 – a version which is one of the longest-playing-time singles in history?

1 The movie *The Lost Boys* featured which Doors song in a version by Echo & The Bunnymen?

2 Which singer appeared as himself in the 1996 movie *Mars Attacks!*?

3 How big is Michael Jackson's 'Neverland' ranch – 2,800 acres, 1,800 acres or 3,300 acres?

4 Donnie Wahlberg was a member of which 1980s/90s band?

5 Written by Mark Knopfler, backed by Jeff Beck on guitar, sung by Tina Turner and released in 1985 – what's the song?

6 The 'disco sound' of the 1970s was given a big boost by which John Travolta movie of 1977?

7 *Cosmo's Factory* was a multi-million seller album by which band?

8 Dr Dre, NWA and Parliament Funkadelic are early exponents of which rap-derived style of music?

9 Which singer died in a skiing accident near Lake Tahoe in January 1998?

10 What is the somewhat more 'cool' rap name of Jeffrey Atkins?

11 What was Ricky Nelson's middle name?

12 In 1998, which (then) 80-year-old won a Grammy for Best Traditional Blues Album with *Don't Look Back*?

13 To which singer was Whitney Houston married between 1992 and 2007?

14 Why was Ozzy Osbourne arrested in 1982 and subsequently banned from the Texas city of San Antonio?

15 *Bella Donna* was the highly successful debut album in 1981 for which singer?

16 Which alternative rock duo from Detroit comprises Meg and Jack White?

1 What was the explosive nickname of pop and country singer Brenda Lee?

2 Andreas Cornelius van Kuijk, born in Holland in 1909, became one of the world's best-known music business managers. By what name is he world famous?

3 Who wrote, and was the first to record, *Blue Suede Shoes*?

4 "On a dark desert highway, cool wind in my hair" is the opening line of which famous song?

5 The single *Wonderwall* was taken from which Oasis album?

6 In 1990, which American rock star was made an unofficial cultural representative by Czech president Vaclav Havel?

7 At which 2004 event did singer Björk appear in a huge dress which represented the sea?

8 Who, together with Janet Jackson, had an unfortunate 'wardrobe malfunction' during the American Superbowl XXVIII halftime show?

9 Which 1960s/70s band featured Signe Anderson and Grace Slick as lead singers at different times?

10 Who, in 2001, became the first female singer to have a No 1 album and a No 1 movie in the same week?

11 Which Michael Jackson album provided the singles *Billie Jean, Wanna Be Startin' Something, Beat It* and *The Girl is Mine*?

12 Who released the album *Back To Black* in 2006?

13 Which singer played the part of Ricky McKinney, opposite Helen Hunt, in the 2000 movie *Pay It Forward*?

14 Which band backed Smokey Robinson from 1965 to 1972?

15 In 2005, who made a comeback with her album *The Emancipation of Mimi*?

16 What was the title of the 2005 hit by The Crazy Frog?

1 What is the title of Snoop Dogg's 2001 autobiography?

2 Zack de la Rocha is the lead singer with which Los Angeles rock band which formed in 1991?

3 *Stuck With You* was a big hit single in 1986 for which band?

4 In 1991, Michael Jackson signed a recording contract with which multi-media company?

5 What nationality are the duo Roxette, who had chart successes in the 1980s and 90s?

6 Which Robert Palmer 1986 No 1 single was very successfully covered by Tina Turner on her *Tina: Live In Europe* album?

7 Which 1961 single by The Marvelettes was covered by, among others, The Beatles, The Carpenters and Shampoo?

8 In which year were all these singles No 1 in the Billboard Top 100: *Escapade* (Janet Jackson); *Vision Of Love* (Mariah Carey); *Step By Step* New (Kids On The Block)?

9 What is the nickname of Red Hot Chili Peppers' guitarist Michael Balzary?

10 Which Bobby Darin single spent nine weeks at No 1 in 1959?

11 Who featured on Flo Rider's smash hit single *Low* in 2008?

12 What was the title of the Santana/Rob Thomas single which was so successful at the end of 1999?

13 In the movie *Ground Hog Day* which famous hit did Bill Murray's character wake up to every morning?

14 *Sunshine Superman*, *Hurdy Gurdy Man* and *Mellow Yellow* were big hits in the 1960s for which folk-rock singer?

15 Sean John Combs is the stage name of which rap singer?

16 What was the odd-ball title by The Bangles which held the No 1 single position at the end of 1986 and start of 1987?

1 Justin Timberlake wrote and performed on which song by the Black Eyed Peas?

2 Which 1992 No 1 hit song by Whitney Houston was written by Dolly Parton and released originally by Parton in 1974?

3 What is the title of Spinal Tap's 1992 album?

4 Which rapper and music producer discovered Eminem?

5 What does BOB stand for on Outkast's 2000 single?

6 Which dance has the less well-known name of Backslide?

7 *Long Haired Lover From Liverpool* was a big hit in the UK in 1972 for which one of the Osmond Brothers?

8 *Tarantula* was the title of a novel written by which rock legend?

9 Who recorded the original version of the song *All I Have To Do Is Dream* in 1958?

10 Which song was rated top in a list of the '500 greatest songs of all time' in *Rolling Stone* magazine in 2004?

11 In *Rolling Stone* magazine's '500 greatest songs of all time', which British band and their song claimed second place?

12 Which jazzman (1901-1971) had hits with *Mack the Knife, When The Saints Go Marching In* and *What A Wonderful World*?

13 *The Hissing Of Summer Lawns* is a classic album, released in 1975, by which singer?

14 *Comme d'habitude* is the original French title of which song, rewritten by Paul Anka and most famously recorded by Frank Sinatra?

15 *The Rose,* a 1979 movie starring Bette Midler as Mary Rose Foster, was loosely based on the life of which rock icon?

16 Which 1998 Van Morrison album shares its title with a *Harry Potter* book?

1   Who played the title role in the 2004 Ray Charles biopic, *Ray*?

2   Which heiress founded Heiress Records in 2004?

3   Which 1995 song by Los Del Rio was voted 'No 1 Greatest One-Hit Wonder Of All Time' by VH1 music channel in 2002?

4   The Californian band Korn is often credited with the creation of which sub-genre of metal music?

5   In the 1980s, the first music video to be aired by MTV was *Video Killed The Radio Star;* performed by which band?

6   Which 1960s rock act's name was adopted after it was allegedly spelled out by a ouija board?

7   What object is the name of heavy metal band Iron Maiden based on?

8   The famous songs *Wichita Lineman, MacArthur Park* and *By The Time I Get To Phoenix* were all written by which man?

9 Possibly her best-known song, which 1967 Aretha Franklin release was adopted as an anthem by some feminist movements?

10 Which song by Procol Harum was a massive hit in the UK in 1967, but waited until its rerelease in 1972 to get to No 6 in America?

11 The hard rock band Brides Of Destruction was formed by Nikki Sixx after the breaking up of which band?

12 What was the middle name of Nirvana's Kurt Cobain?

13 *Beauty And The Beat* (sic) was the hit debut album for which Californian girl band?

14 Which 1966 Supremes No 1 hit single was covered by Phil Collins, whose version reached No 10 in 1983?

15 "Let us be lovers, we'll marry our fortunes together" are the opening lyrics of which Simon and Garfunkel song?

16 Who killed Marvin Gaye in 1984?

1　Which rapper, who died from AIDS in 1995, established the Ruthless Records label?

2　What does the 'J' stand for in the name of Mary J Blige?

3　*Sympathy For The Devil,* a song originally by the Rolling Stones, was covered by which band for the movie *Interview With The Vampire*?

4　On January 1st 2000, Prince played which of his songs live in New York, vowing never to play it again?

5　Which rock and blues rock band is comprised of Dusty Hill, Frank Beard and Billy Gibbons?

6　In 2004, rapper Kanye West won three Grammys for which debut album?

7　What is the weird title of U2's three-times-platinum album of 2004?

8　In 1996, with which backing group was Gladys Knight inducted into the Rock and Roll Hall of Fame?

9 Which singer has earned the titles 'Hardest-Working Man In Showbusiness' and 'King Of Funk'?

10 Washington DC-based Chuck Brown is known as 'The Godfather of …' which music genre?

11 Which song was a No 2 hit for Ray Charles in 1962 and a No 1 Country hit for Mickey Gilley in 1981?

12 Which band takes its name from the title of a novel by Herman Hesse?

13 Rapper Ice Cube appeared in which 1991 Academy Award-nominated movie?

14 *The Slip,* an album released in 2008, was the seventh studio album by which rock band?

15 The 2007 Grammy Album Of The Year award was taken by which Dixie Chicks album?

16 Whose album *Supernatural* was the first Grammy Album Of The Year of the third millennium?

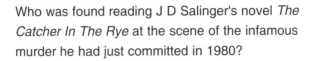

1 Who was found reading J D Salinger's novel *The Catcher In The Rye* at the scene of the infamous murder he had just committed in 1980?

2 In 2008, who had a big hit with the single *I Kissed A Girl* from her album *One Of The Boys*?

3 *Raising Sand* was a 2007 collaboration album between Robert Plant and which female singer?

4 *An American Prayer* was the last studio album to be released by which band?

5 The best-selling single of the 1980s, *Physical* was performed by which songstress?

6 Who had No 1 hit singles with *Take A Bow* in 2008, and *Umbrella* in 2007?

7 What is the better-known name of rapper Christopher George Latore Wallace?

8 Which star of many horror movies provided a voice part in Michael Jackson's *Thriller*?

9 In 1976, why did Bruce Springsteen climb over the wall of Elvis Presley's Graceland home in the middle of the night?

10 *Honky Chateau* was the first American No 1 album for which singer?

11 Whose *Rockin' Around The Christmas Tree* has reached the American charts at least 11 times since its first release in 1960?

12 The single *Drive,* from their album *Heartbeat City,* was the highest chart position release for which 1970s/80s band?

13 *Nothing Compares 2 U*, a massive worldwide hit in 1990 for Sinead O'Connor, was penned by which American singer/songwriter?

14 The band Air, who released the album *Pocket Symphony* in 2007, come from which country?

15 Bobby Hatfield and Bill Medley were the two halves of which pop duo?

16 *I Get Around* was the first American No 1 single for which band in 1964?

1 Mary Travers, Noel Stookey and Peter Yarrow were known collectively by which stage name?

2 Which band's first American No 1 album was the 1975 *Gratitude*?

3 Which Anglo-American band, first popular in the 1980s, released the albums *Learning To Crawl* and *Get Close*?

4 *Thirteen Tales From Urban Bohemia* was the third album by which band?

5 *Until It's Time For You To Go*, a song recorded by Elvis Presley, Barbra Streisand, Neil Diamond and others, was written by which singer/songwriter?

6 Which American band's greatest success is the single from 1993, *Into Your Arms*?

7 Which car manufacturer was concerned at the Beastie Boys' use of its logo as a medallion, fearing that BB fans would steal them from its cars?

8 An R&B exponent, singer/songwriter and famed guitar legend; who names his guitars 'Lucille'?

9 *Smells Like Nirvana* and *Achy Breaky Song* are parodies on original songs by which musician and satirist?

10 *Islands In The Stream* was a 1983 country music No 1 hit for which male and female duo?

11 Which popular band took its name from an Austrian archduke who was assassinated in 1914?

12 Sean Kinney is the long-term drummer with which Seattle-based band?

13 Born James Smith in Texas 1938, who had chart successes in the 1960s with *Hold Me* and *Somewhere?*

14 Justin Timberlake, Christina Aguilera and Britney Spears each had early successes with appearances on which American TV show?

15 *Independent Women Part 1* by Destiny's Child was used in which movie of 2000?

16 Born Gordon Sumner, how did Sting get his stage name?

1 Which *Star Trek* major cast member has recorded campy cover versions of *Lucy In The Sky With Diamonds* and *Mr Tambourine Man*?

2 *I Am Woman,* a single released in 1972, was significant because it was the first to reach the American No 1 position by a woman of what nationality?

3 Which singer used four alter egos (Pip, Santa, Clyde and Isabel) for her album *American Doll Posse*?

4 *Maggie May/Reason To Believe* was the first American No 1 single for which singer?

5 *Brown Sugar* was the first track on the album *Sticky Fingers,* by which band?

6 Who performed his last concert in Indianapolis on June 26 1977?

7 Covered by dozens of artists, who wrote, and first recorded, the classic song *Ain't No Sunshine*?

8 Which Pink Floyd song was banned in South Africa because it was taken up as an anthem by anti-apartheid protesters?

9 Whose American top ten chart breakthrough came in 1972 with *School's Out*?

10 Although written and first recorded by Bob Marley, whose cover of *I Shot The Sheriff* was the most successful in America?

11 Which singer started her career as the drummer in all-girl punk band The Germs, then went on to sing with the Go Gos?

12 Who wrote the song *Who Knows Where The Time Goes,* covered by many artists including Nina Simone, Judy Collins and Nanci Griffith?

13 Which singer won the first American Idol competition in 2002?

14 Which soul/disco singer founded the Love Unlimited Orchestra?

15 Which Detroit-based band has the alternative name of The Wild Bunch?

16 Lenny Kravitz and Ingrid Chavez, together with the singer herself, co-wrote *Justify My Love;* who performed it?

1   *Rapper's Delight* by the Sugarhill Gang was the first record of which music genre to win a gold disc award in 1979?

2   Which song holds the world record for the most cover versions, the original dating from 1965?

3   Which pop/rock veteran used to be the frontman with The Velvet Underground?

4   *Definitely Maybe* was the first album to be released by which band in 1994?

5   *I Got The*, by Labi Siffre, was sampled on which Eminem release of 1999?

6   Which former member of The Beatles died on November 29th 2001?

7   *Music For Supermarkets* is unique in that only one copy was made. Which performer released this in 1983?

8   "God had to create disco music so that I could be born" is a quotation attributed to which performer?

9   *Morning Train,* a US No 1 hit for Sheena Easton, had which original UK title? It was changed for its American release because a Dolly Parton song with the same title had been previously released.

10   Cy Curnin of the band Fixx appeared in which Tina Turner music video?

11   *I Want That Man* and *Two Times Blue* were solo singles by which former band fronter?

12   Which Henry Mancini song from the movie *Breakast At Tiffany's* became Andy Williams' theme song?

13   Which movie/TV composer marred Bridget Fonda in 2003?

14   *Solitude Standing* is the most successful album of which singer/songwriter?

15   Which hit song, originally by The Drifters, was covered by movie actor Bruce Willis?

16   *Wake Me Up Before You Go Go* was a 1984 breakthrough single for which band?

1. Who had his first No 1 single with *You Send Me* in 1957, although he is possibly more famous for *Chain Gang* of 1960?

2. Jefferson Airplane's *White Rabbit* was based on which classic novel by Lewis Carroll?

3. In 1990, which soul singer was paralyzed from the neck down after he was hit by falling equipment on stage at a concert in New York?

4. Which Nirvana album has a yellow toy duck on the back cover?

5. What was the title of Nirvana's final album, released in 1993?

6. *A Matter Of Life And Death* was the 2006 album by which heavy metal band who have been around since 1975?

7. What is the common theme which runs through k.d. lang's album *Drag*?

8. What was the title of the 2005 debut album by Rihanna?

9   Which song recorded by Otis Redding, while sounding finished, was actually not completed to his satisfaction on his untimely death in 1967?

10   What is the better-known stage name of rapper/songwriter/producer Timothy Z Mosley?

11   Whose sixth solo album was the 2005 *Cookbook*?

12   Which soul/R&B singer, associated with The Drifters, co-wrote the song *Stand By Me*?

13   Which 1997 single by Elton John was released as a result of the death of Diana, Princess of Wales?

14   Guns n' Roses was partly formed by members of which band with a similar-sounding name?

15   *Kiss And Say Goodbye* was a 1976 worldwide hit single by which band?

16   In 2001, shortly after completing her video *Rock The Boat*, which singer died in an airplane crash in the Bahamas?

1 Which was the only Buddy Holly (as lead singer with The Crickets) single to reach No 1 in America?

2 Which band's 2007 album is entitled *Unbreakable*?

3 What was the title of Hootie And The Blowfish's debut album?

4 Which movie soundtrack album of 1977 became one of the biggest-selling of all time, going platinum 15 times in America?

5 Whose career took off with *I'm Every Woman* in 1978 and continues to thrive in 2008 with *One For All Time*?

6 *The Woman In Red*, a 1980s movie starring Gene Wilder, featured songs by Stevie Wonder and which female singing star?

7 Which album and single by Paul McCartney and Wings reached No 1 in America in 1974?

8 Which band's successes included the singles *Monkey Gone To Heaven, Here Comes Your Man* and *Head On*?

9 Which American guitarist/singer devised the 'Duckwalk'?

10 The 2001 No 1 single *Butterfly* and the album *Darkhorse* are the highlights of which band's discography?

11 In 2004, which band's album *Fallen* was Grammy nominated but didn't win? However, the band did win Best New Artist and Best Hard Rock Performance.

12 To which British musician was Diana Krall married in 2003?

13 Which Canadian rock band's second album, *All Killer No Filler,* scored high in America in 2001?

14 In which American city did the Band Aid concert of 1985 take place?

15 Whose *In The Year 2525* was a great hit (No 1 in the US for six weeks) in the year 1969?

16 Although not a big hit at the time, *Christmas Wrapping* of 1981 continues to be popular around the world in the 2000s. Which band was it by?

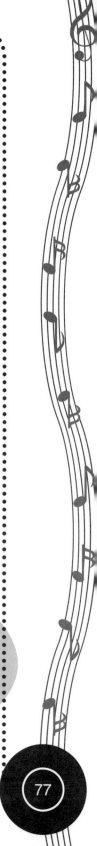

1 What is the title of Twisted Sister's Christmas album?

2 Complete the name of the band: Booker T and ___?

3 Which duo performed originally under the name of Caesar and Cleo?

4 Which singer is the daughter of Nat King Cole?

5 Which British punk band's greatest American success was the single *Rock The Casbah* from the album *Combat Rock*?

6 What do the abbreviations in the stage name 'L L Cool J' stand for?

7 Whose critically acclaimed four-disc set *Fruit Tree* was originally released (posthumously) in 1986 and rereleased in 2007?

8 What is the stage name of Josh Davis, whose 1996 debut album *Entroducing* is comprised mostly of samples?

9   *Lovely Day*, the well-known song by Bill Withers, has a claim to fame for having the longest what?

10   Which singer has had major successes with *Hollaback Girl* and *The Sweet Escape*?

11   Cuba has condemned western popular music as 'decadent' for decades, but which British band played there in 2001, the first to do so for more than 20 years?

12   *We Are The World* by ad hoc 'superband' USA For Africa, was written by which two famous singers?

13   Which Los Angeles landmark was the title of Richard Harris' seven-minute-long big hit in 1968?

14   "I am just a poor boy, but my story's seldom told" are the opening lyrics to which Paul Simon song?

15   Which drummer with The Who died from a drugs overdose in 1978?

16   Which British band took its name from a 19th century Paris commune which occupied the city after the Franco-Prussian war?

1 In 1973, ten years after her death, who was the first woman to be inducted into the Country Music Hall Of Fame?

2 What was the first No 1 hit single by the Red Hot Chili Peppers?

3 Why wasn't Tupac Shakur able to go out on the town and celebrate on the success of his album *Me Against The World* when it reached No 1 in 1995?

4 Whose solo album *Bare* reached No 4 in America in 2003?

5 Freddie Mercury and opera singer Montserrat Caballé duetted on which song – a theme song to the Olympic Games of 1988?

6 *How You Sell Soul To A Soulless People Who Sold Their Soul?* is the lengthy title of which band's tenth album, released in 2007?

7 What was the nationality of the band Los Bravos, who had a worldwide hit, *Black Is Black,* in 1966?

8 Which Texas-based 23-member 'choral symphonic rock' group was founded in 2000?

9 Betty Hutton, of early movie fame, recorded a song entitled *Blow A Fuse* in the 1950s. In 1995, who covered the song under the title *It's Oh So Quiet*?

10 Which Californian hard rock band is fronted by Jesse 'The Devil' Hughes?

11 Complete the title of the 2007 album from Electric Six: *I Shall Exterminate Everything Around Me ...*

12 *Absolution* and *Black Holes And Revelations* are albums by which British alternative rock band?

13 Which pop and country singer released her seventh album *Perfectly Clear* in 2008?

14 *Give Us Your Poor* is a 2007 compilation album with songs from Bruce Springsteen, Pete Seeger, Keb Mo, and others. Its charitable aim is to aid which kind of social problem?

15 Who released his songs-for-children album *All Aboard* just prior to his accidental death in 1997?

16 In 1995, with whom did Bryan Adams duet on the song (written with Gretchen Peters) *Rock Steady*?

1   *Grandes Luces De Fuego,* by OV7, a Mexican pop band, was a rendition in Spanish of which Jerry Lee Lewis hit?

2   *Happy Together*, of 1967, was possibly the biggest hit for which band?

3   Which Abba recording was sampled on Madonna's 2005 single *Hung Up*?

4   From which European country did the 'black metal' band Mayhem originate?

5   From which band did Phil Collins quit to go solo in 1981?

6   What was the final song Elvis Presley sang at his last live concert appearance in 1977?

7   The Beatles song, *With A Little Help From My Friends* was very successfully covered in a 1969 bluesy version by which solo artist?

8   *Games People Play*, a song covered by many artists, including Dolly Parton, was written and originally released by which singer in 1968?

9 Who played the title role in the 1979 made-for-TV movie *Elvis*?

10 *When A Man Loves a Woman* was the biggest-selling single for which American blues/R&B singer?

11 Bing Crosby's *White Christmas* had the reputation of being the biggest-selling single ever, until overtaken by which Elton John single?

12 Which Prince song led to the introduction of the Parental Advisory warning sticker being placed on certain (ie explicit) record and video covers?

13 Which alternative rock band's second album was entitled *Version 2.0*?

14 *Decksandrumsandrockandroll* was the 1998 debut album of which band?

15 Who declined to record *Son Of A Preacher Man* in 1969, leaving a big opportunity for Dusty Springfield, who scored a big hit with the song?

16 The singles *Krafty* and *Jetstream* are taken from *Waiting For The Siren's Call*, a 2005 album by which band?

1 Which American female singer was the youngest person ever to win a Grammy Award (aged 14) in 1996?

2 Which album by Cher was the best-selling, worldwide, of 1998?

3 Which Seattle rock band's excessively long name is often reduced to PUSA?

4 In 1993, Eddie Vedder of Pearl Jam appeared on the front of which magazine, as part of its featured story on the popularity of grunge music?

5 What was the big song and part-animated music video success of 1985 that brought international fame for the band A-Ha?

6 *Not Ready To Make Nice* took the 2007 Grammy Award for Best Song for which band?

7 *American Idiot* was the 2004 multi-platinum album by which Californian band?

8 *Spider Pig* was a quirky number from the soundtrack of which 2007 animated movie?

9 To whom was Paul Simon married between 1983 and 1984?

10 The 1972 Academy Award for Best Original Song went to Isaac Hayes for which movie tune?

11 Who, from the age of 15, studied classical piano and also conducted the choir at Howard University, before her singing career took off with the 1969 album *First Take*?

12 In 1992, a photograph of which personage was ripped up by Sinead O'Connor on the *Saturday Night Live* TV show?

13 *Stay*, a 1992 single from the album *Hormonally Yours* was the biggest hit for which female duo?

14 *And A Voice To Sing With* is the autobiography of which folk music singer?

15 *This Is Me Then* is a 2002 album by which singer?

16 *So Amazing: An All-Star Tribute To...* is a collection of songs by various artists originally performed by, and in tribute to, which singer who died in 2005?

1 Formed by brothers Ron and Russell Mael in Los Angeles in 1970, which band released its 20th studio album, *Hello Young Lovers*, in 2006?

2 Which song by Pink Floyd concerns the theft of ladies' underwear; the thief being the man named in the song's title?

3 *One More Saturday Night* was a 2006 release by which 1950s-style band whose movie appearances include *Grease* and *Festival Express*?

4 The accidental burning down of which Swiss city's casino, during a Frank Zappa concert, is the subject of Deep Purple's song *Smoke On The Water*?

5 What was the title of Beyoncé Knowles' debut solo album?

6 *Labels or Love* by Fergie, *All Dressed In Love* by Jennifer Hudson, and *New York Girls* by Morningwood all feature in which 2008 movie?

7 How many Bob Dylan American No 1 singles have there been?

8 In the movie *Top Gun,* which famous song was performed by the band Berlin?

9   *Bright Lights, Big City,* a 1988 movie starring Michael J Fox and Kiefer Sutherland, featured music written by which ex-member of Steely Dan?

10   What is the nationality of Guess Who?

11   *The Other Side Of Summer* from his album *Mighty Like A Rose* is by which British artist?

12   Which traditional New Orleans blues song was a No 1 hit for The Animals in 1964 and a No 7 for Frijid Pink in 1970?

13   Which singer played Foxxy Cleopatra in the Austin Powers movie *Goldmember*?

14   In which movie, starring Hugh Grant and Sandra Bullock, did singer Norah Jones appear as herself?

15   In April 2006, which American singer was found dead (of natural causes) in his hotel room in Cardiff, Wales?

16   What was the first single by The Beatles to reach No 1 in the USA?

1 What was the last single by The Beatles to reach No 1 in the USA while all members of the band were alive?

2 In 1970, George Harrison and Ravi Shankar were the organizers of which huge event in New York to raise money for the victims of an Asian hurricane?

3 What do the following No 1 hit songs all have in common? *To Know Him Is To Love Him, He's A Rebel, You've Lost That Lovin' Feelin', My Sweet Lord.*

4 *Outlandos d'Amour* was the American breakthrough album of which band in 1979?

5 Lyrics from which Neil Young song were quoted in Kurt Cobain's suicide note?

6 Which Scottish band, popular in the 1980s, shares its name with the title of a Western movie of 1958, starring Gregory Peck?

7 Complete the name of the band: Grandmaster Flash and ___?

8 *Back To Life (However Do You Want Me)* from the album *Club Classics Vol 1* was a hit for which act?

9 What is the stage name of rapper and former record company CEO Shawn Corey Carter?

10 Which rap artist's *You Make Me Wanna* featured in the charts for a long period during 1997/98?

11 Which disco/funk band's greatest successes were the singles *I Want Your Love, Le Freak* and *Good Times*?

12 'The Father Of Chicago Blues' is a name given to which blues singer/songwriter?

13 The girl trio Wilson Phillips are the offspring of people from which 1960s bands?

14 Which rock band, whose name is the same as that of a heroic native American, have been associated with Neil Young since the late 1960s?

15 Which band takes its name from a dream-associated sleep condition?

16 Which San Francisco band had their first hit with the single *Do You Believe In Love* from their album *Picture This*?

1 Although he went solo for a time in his later career, which band did Peter Noone front for several years in the 1960s and 1970s?

2 Led Zeppelin's *The Battle Of Evermore* was a folk-style ballad which appeared on their fourth album in 1971. To which novel (recently made into a trilogy of movies) did the song allude?

3 Which singer, once married to Carly Simon, had a bridge in North Carolina named after him?

4 To which multi-national coffee-house chain does the record label 'Hear Music' belong?

5 Also the title of one of his biggest-selling albums, which musician has the nickname 'Slowhand'?

6 Prince's *Alphabet Street* is a single taken from which of his albums?

7 Whose 1966 album *Wildest Organ In Town* was rereleased in 2004, two years before his death?

8 What does the 'WA' stand for in the band name NWA?

9 Whose *Jagged Little Pill* album *has* sold over fourteen million units in the USA alone?

10 Which record label has used a portrait of a dog named Nipper on its albums, etc, for more than one hundred years?

11 Whose album *The Rise And Fall Of Ziggy Stardust And The Spiders From Mars* made the American charts in 1972?

12 *One Day It Will Please Us To Remember Even This* is the long title of which long-running American band's 2006 album?

13 Which British girl band had a big hit with *Venus* in 1986?

14 Which American psychodelic rock band's lengthy name is sometimes reduced to BJM?

15 From which country does the girl band The 5.6.7.8's originate?

16 Which female rock artist was the leader of the band The Pretenders?

1 Who sang *Wand'rin' Star* from the soundtrack of the 1970 movie *Paint Your Wagon,* a single which made a surprising No 1 in the UK?

2 *Breakfast In America* was a big success for which 1970s band?

3 Which classic Led Zeppelin album cover features the facade of old tenements with the album's name spelled out in the windows of the buildings?

4 *Love.Angel.Music.Baby* was the debut solo album of which singer?

5 What was the collective name of Posh, Scary, Sporty, Ginger and Baby?

6 The front cover of which album by the band No Doubt features a girl in a red dress against a background that suggests a failed harvest?

7 Which San Francisco garage rock band released their album *Stop Drop And Roll* in 2008?

8 The bands Kings Of Convenience and Broken Social Scene were home to which Canadian singer who released her third solo album *The Reminder* in 2007?

9 Which album by Bob Marley and the Wailers was, in 1998, hailed by Time Magazine as the greatest of the 20th century?

10 Whose solo career began with the album *The Block Is Hot* in 1999?

11 Who released his album *Trilla* in 2008?

12 Which Kanye West album won Best Rap Album at the 2005 Grammy Awards?

13 Several members of which band died in an airplane crash when the plane ran out of fuel over Mississippi in October 1977?

14 What title is common to a 1997 movie starring Joshua Schaefer, a 2007 TV sitcom and a Beatles' song?

15 Chris Martin, who has played rhythm guitar for Coldplay and appears on Kanye West's album *Graduation,* is married to which movie actress?

16 Corin Tucker and Carrie Brownstein were the two halves of which band who released their last album *Into The Woods* in 2005?

1 *SexyBack* was a No 1 hit single from which 2006 album by Justin Timberlake?

2 In 1992, the management of the Cleveland Orchestra took legal action against Sony Music over unauthorized sampling, on Michael Jackson's album *Dangerous,* of a 1961 recording of the music of which composer?

3 The classic song *Wherever I Lay My Hat (That's My Home)* was part-written and first recorded by which singer?

4 Which band's biggest American hits have been with the albums *Evil Heat* and *Riot City Blues*?

5 *Money For Nothing*, taken from their equally successful album *Brothers In Arms*, was a phenomenal hit for which band?

6 The Miami Sound Machine are famous as the backing band to which female singing star?

7 *Surf City* was the first No 1 single for which duo?

8 *No One Knows* is a No 1 single taken from which album by Queens of the Stone Age?

9 *Feeling Good* has been covered by dozens of acts since it first appeared in 1965, including a version on which album by the Pussycat Dolls?

10 *Gimme Some More* and *Break Ya Neck* were two hits by which hip-hop and rap star?

11 Which hip-hop/rap star originally fronted the band A Tribe Called Quest until it broke up 1998, thereafter pursuing a solo career?

12 Which Bob Dylan song was a big hit in 1965 for both The Byrds and Cher?

13 Which 1960s trio made a big impression in the UK and other countries, but less so in America, with hits including *The Sun Ain't Gonna Shine Anymore*?

14 Which famous single by Queen had *I'm In Love With My Car* as the B-side?

15 What was the title of the last album by The Doors, released just before the death of Jim Morrison in 1971?

16 What is the stage name of John Joseph Lydon?

1   What was the title of Jeff Buckley's debut album of 1994?

2   *Greetings From Asbury Park* was the debut album of which singer?

3   What was the title of Bon Jovi's earliest really successful album, which reached No 1 in 1986?

4   *Hot Fuss* was the highly successful first studio album of which band?

5   The multi music-genre singer Damien Rice comes from which country?

6   What was the title of Michael Jackson's fifth album, released in 1979?

7   *Tomorrow Never Knows* is the final track on which highly influential Beatles album of 1966?

8   *You Could Have It So Much Better* was the second album, released in 2006, by which British band?

9 The band Satellite Party was formed by Perry Farrell, formerly of Porno For Pyros and which other band?

10 *The Living Room Tour* is a 2005 live album by which singer/songwriter?

11 J D Fortune became the lead singer of which band after he won the position in a TV competition in 2005?

12 Which solo singer joined the Jackson 5 to create the 1974 No 1 hit single *You Haven't Done Nothin'*?

13 *There's A Riot Goin' On* was the highest chart position (No 1) album of which band?

14 Which singer floated away on her 'Drowned World' tour in 2001?

15 Which classic Rolling Stones album featured *Rocks Off* on the first track and *Soul Survivor* on the last?

16 *Wish* was the most successful album for which rock band, reaching No 2 in America in 1992?

1   *Last Train To Clarkesville* was the first No 1 hit single for which 1960s band?

2   The 'Twist' dance craze of the early 1960s was the subject of *The Twist* and *Let's Twist Again* – singles by which singer?

3   *Achtung Baby* was the biggest selling album (eight million units) in America for which band?

4   Which road did Elton John say "goodbye" to in 1973?

5   Which classic album spent over seven months at the top of the American charts and received a Grammy for Best Album in 1977?

6   What is the title of the 2006 music reference book by Robert Dimery which lists a multitude of recommended albums from Frank Sinatra to White Stripes?

7   According to the title of Neil Young's 1979 album, what doesn't rust do?

8   Whose 'Bigger Bang Tour' was the subject of a 2008 documentary movie directed by Martin Scorsese?

9   Which musician founded the Area Festivals, the first of which took place in 2001?

10   Which theatrical act produced the satirical *Rock Concert Instruction Manual*?

11   Which female singer's hit albums include *Hounds Of Love, The Sensual World* and *The Red Shoes*?

12   Where do the alternative rock band The Cranberries originate from?

13   With which 1972 single did Michael Jackson first reach No 1 in the US charts?

14   Which R&B/soul singer originally sang with the band Rufus?

15   In 2003, who was voted 'Greatest Guitarist Of All Time' by *Rolling Stone* magazine?

16   What is the stage name of Don Glen Vliet?

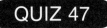

1 To which group of instruments do the piano, the organ and the Moog synthesiser belong?

2 *My Name Is Buddy* is a 2007 concept album by which singer and guitar veteran?

3 Which band, fronted by Bob Geldof, is probably most famous for the hit single *I Don't Like Mondays*?

4 To which singer was actress/model Julianne Phillips married from 1985 to 1989?

5 In 1983, *Owner Of A Lonely Heart* gave which band its only No 1 single in the US Hot 100?

6 Which band was formed by Iggy Pop in 1967, and although disbanded in 1974, was re-formed in 2003?

7 What is the name by which musician and composer Evangelos Odysseas Papathanassiou is better known?

8 *Just Because,* from their album *Strays,* was the last big hit for which band before their breakup in 2004?

9 *BloodSugarSexMagic,* the 1991 album by Red Hot Chili Peppers, produced which No 1 single for the band?

10 *Lady Sings The Blues,* a biographical movie based on the life of Billie Holiday, starred which singer?

11 Which veteran singer covered Glenn Miller's *At Last* in her famous version of 1961?

12 How many Grammy awards were won by Alicia Keys in 2002?

13 What is the better known stage name of Curtis James Jackson III?

14 Which rap artist featured on Jennifer Lopez' single *All I Have*?

15 Which heavy metal band's successful albums include *Rest In Peace* and *Youthanasia*?

16 In 2004, which progressive/symphonic rock band released *The Lost Christmas Eve,* the third album in their 'Christmas Trilogy' series?

1 Whose single *Lollipop* made it to No 1 in May 2008?

2 Which trio of solo singers produced the 2008 smash hit single *Love In This Club Part II*?

3 Which band took its title from the names of the two founding members plus the title of a magazine devoted to truckers?

4 After finding that their song *I Disappear* was being made available illegally via an internet file sharer, which band sued the company in 2000?

5 For which James Bond movie did Carly Simon perform the title song *Nobody Does It Better*?

6 In which year was Madonna born?

7 What is the title of the 2008 documentary movie, written, narrated and produced by Madonna, concerning the plight of African children?

8 Which band was named after a priestess who appeared in several episodes of *Star Trek*?

9 Which band shares its name with the title of a 1950 multi-award winning movie starring Bette Davis and Anne Baxter?

10 In which year was Mariah Carey born?

11 The band Sigur Ros originate from which country?

12 Who had a smash hit with *Ice Ice Baby* in 1990?

13 Which band includes members Babydaddy and Paddy Boom?

14 Bob Siebenberg (aka Bob C Benberg) was the American member of which British superband?

15 Who was Capitol Records' 1956 answer to RCA's Elvis Presley? His best-known song is probably *Be-Bop-A-Lula*.

16 *Daydream, Nashville Cats* and *Summer In The City* were all hit singles for which band in the 1960s?

1 Which song by Queen shares its title with that of a novel by Mark Helprin and a play by William Shakespeare?

2 In 1978, New York-born Jeff Wayne released which concept album, based on a novel by H G Wells?

3 Recordings taken from which band's 2007 'Turn It On Again' reunion tour were turned into a live album, *Live Over Europe*?

4 Which 1970s band's greatest hit was *Make It With You*?

5 What is the better known professional name of musician/songwriter/producer Alan Kuperschmidt?

6 Which classic album was voted top place in Rolling Stone magazine's '500 Greatest Albums Of All Time' list in 2003?

7 Which classic album was voted second place in Rolling Stone magazine's '500 Greatest Albums Of All Time' list in 2003?

8 With six weeks at the top of the singles chart in 1979, *My Sharona* is probably the best known song of which band?

9 Which band was named after a German art and craft movement founded by the architect Walter Gropius?

10 Which Goffin/King song was a big hit for The Drifters in 1962 and was covered by Neil Diamond in 1993?

11 *What's New Pussycat,* the title song to the movie of the same name, sung by Tom Jones, was penned by which songwriting duo?

12 *If Not For You,* penned by Bob Dylan, found its greatest success in whose version of 1971?

13 Of which rock band was Van Morrison the front man before he went solo in 1966?

14 Who, in 1972, was replaced by Billy Griffin as lead singer with the Motown band The Miracles?

15 In 2003, who spent nine weeks at the top of the Billboard Hot 100 with *In Da Club*?

16 *In The Year 2525* by Zager and Evans was at the top of the Billboard singles chart at the time of which great event of 1969?

1 What was the Billboard Hot 100 No 1 single at Christmas and New Year 2007?

2 What was the first Billboard Hot 100 No 1 single of the 21st century?

3 What are Janet Jackson's middle names?

4 Who teamed up with R Kelly on the 1998 No 1 hit *I'm Your Angel*?

5 Which appropriately titled single by Barenaked Ladies spent a short time at the No 1 slot in 1999?

6 Which band's name derives from a 1960 movie starring Robert Wagner and Natalie Wood?

7 What name was used by record producer Norman Smith, most famous for his 1972 big hit *Oh Babe What Would You Say*?

8 In 2008, who overtook Elvis Presley's previously unbroken record for the greatest number of No 1 records in the American Billboard charts?

9 Which band had hits in the 1960s with *Mony Mony* and *Crimson And Clover*?

10 Whose American successes have included the singles *When The Going Gets Tough The Tough Get Going* and *There'll Be Sad Songs*?

11 Born in 1936 and dying aged 52, he had his fair share of tragedy; losing his first wife in a motorcycle accident in 1966 and two of his sons when his house burned down in 1968. Who was he?

12 *When You're In Love With A Beautiful Woman* was a 1979 Top Ten hit for which band?

13 *Still Crazy After All These Years* was a 1975 album by which artist?

14 Which long-established band produced the hit single *Does Anybody Really Know What Time It Is*?

15 The South African Ladysmith Black Mambazo band came to worldwide attention after it featured on which Paul Simon album?

16 Which band was formed from four individuals who responded to an ad in the LA *Daily Variety* in 1965?

1 Which Funkadelic album was recorded in 1984 but not released until 2007?

2 Which band had their 1990 Grammy award revoked after it was found that the band's members were not the ones performing on 'their' single *All Or Nothing*?

3 Who played bass guitar with the Rolling Stones from 1962 till 1993?

4 *Pocketful Of Sunshine,* from her album of the same name made the American Top Ten in May 2008 for which singer?

5 Which band comprised an American, Lady Miss Kier; a Ukrainian, Super DJ Dmitri; and a Japanese, Towa Tei?

6 Which singer, who was dubbed 'The Female Elvis', died in 2007, aged 67?

7 *Lost In Love* and *Making Love Out Of Nothing At All* were big hit singles for which band?

8 Beach Boys Carl Wilson and Bruce Johnston sang backing vocals on which Elton John single?

9 Warren Beatty, Kris Kristofferson and Mick Jagger are all possible contenders for the subject of which song by Carly Simon?

10 Which British singer, who had several hits in the 1970s, converted to Islam in 1977 – changing his name to Yusuf Islam? He was turned back on a flight from London to Washington in 2004 because his 'new' name aroused suspicion with the FBI.

11 "Like a movie scene in the sweetest dreams" are the opening lyrics of which Jennifer Lopez song?

12 The Bee Gees broke up after the sudden death of which of the brothers in 2003?

13 Which Cuban-born singer used to work as a Spanish and French language translator in Miami?

14 Which famous guitarist produced instrumentals such as *Rebel Rouser* and *Because They're Young*?

15 Whose *Ain't Nothin' Goin' On But The Rent* had chart success in 1986?

16 Which band's greatest success was the 1996 album *The Score,* selling over 18 million copies worldwide?

1 To which musician was Bob Dylan's *Song To Woody* dedicated?

2 In 1971-72 two members of which band were killed in separate motorcycle accidents, one year apart, at almost the same location in Macon, Georgia?

3 Bob Dylan teamed up with which band to record *The Basement Tapes*?

4 Which two Bee Gees wrote the classic standard song *To Love Somebody*?

5 Which band performed the 1970 hit *Come And Get It*, featured in the movie *The Magic Christian*?

6 Who released her first album, *No Angel,* in 1999 and her second, *Life For Rent,* in 2003?

7 What is the nationality of R&B/soul/hip hop singer Jamelia?

8 Which country singer/songwriter added 43 years to his life when he gave up his seat on the fateful Buddy Holly airplane which crashed in February 1959?

9   What was the title of the 1983 debut solo album that propelled Cyndi Lauper to super-stardom?

10   Later released as a single that became a big hit for the band, which Paul Simon song featured on the Lemonheads' album *It's A Shame About Ray*?

11   *Harper Valley PTA* was a major hit single for which country singer in 1968?

12   *Shadowland* was the 1988 debut solo album of which singer?

13   The albums *Songs From The Last Century*, *Older* and *Listen Without Prejudice* are all by which artist?

14   The rap trio Naughty by Nature scored a big hit with the single *O.P.P.* Which Jackson 5 song was sampled in the production of this record?

15   Which album by Sonic Youth shares its title with that of a Creedence Clearwater Revival single?

16   Joachim Krauledat escaped from East Germany in the 1940s and changed his name to John Kay to eventually become the front man of which famous rock band?

1   John Fogerty, who released a new solo album, *Revival,* in 2007, was a member of which 1960s band?

2   Who played the Acid Queen in the movie version of The Who rock opera, *Tommy*?

3   Anita, Ruth and Issa are the members of which rock/R&B trio?

4   Released in 2008, *Third* is the fourth album of which British band, whose preceding album, *Roseland NYC Live,* appeared in 1998?

5   *Sorry Ma, Forgot To Take Out The Trash* was the intriguing title of the first album by which band?

6   Complete the line-up: Junior Walker and the ...?

7   Amy Ray and Emily Saliers are the two halves of which folk rock duo?

8   *La Vie En Rose, Do Or Die* and *I Need A Man* were all big disco-dance hits for which six-feet tall model-turned singer?

9 Where did the 'Devil go down to' in the Charlie Daniels Band hit song of 1979?

10 Which band's already infamous reputation reached a new level when its members appeared naked on stage at the 1993 Lollapalooza festival in protest at the Parents' Music Resource Centre?

11 The 2001 album, *Twisted Forever*, which included songs by Anthrax, Chuck D and Overkill, was a tribute to which band by their record company?

12 Which country singer has received Grammy awards for *The Whisky Ain't Workin'* (1992) and *Same Old Train* (1998)?

13 The Connie Francis hits *Stupid Cupid* and *Where The Boys Are* were written by which well-known singer?

14 *Follow The Leader* was the third album, and the first to make it to No 1, by which heavy metal band?

15 *The Drugs Don't Work* was a hit single from the album *Urban Hymns,* by which band?

16 Which singer appeared, as herself, in the *Spiderman* movie (2002) and *Scary Movie 3* (2003)?

1   *Two Sides Of The Moon* was the first solo album of which former major band member?

2   Which American band released the album *Recycler* in 1990?

3   Which Australian band released the album *Full Moon, Dirty Hearts* in 1993?

4   World famous for his *Tubular Bells,* who created the album *Songs Of Distant Earth,* based on a science fiction novel by Arthur C Clarke?

5   Released in 1997, *Be Here Now* is the title of which band's third studio album?

6   Which 1997 album from Radiohead scored an American double platinum?

7   What title is common to a 1995 album by Blur, a 1963 World War II movie starring Steve McQueen and a song by Boys Like Girls?

8   Who is *The Force Behind The Power* with her 1991 solo album?

9 Which American superband featured on Neil Young's *Mirror Ball* album?

10 What reassurance did the Bee Gees give to the world with the title of their 1993 album?

11 Which band had great success with the *Good Stuff* album and single in 1992?

12 What title is common to a 1995 Black Sabbath album and a 2007 album from Christine Dolce?

13 Complete the line up of this clean-cut 1960s band: Jay and the ___.

14 *Forever, For Always, For ...* is a 2004 'various artists' album dedicated to the memory of which soul singer?

15 Who implored us to *Keep The Faith* with his 1992 album?

16 Which singer complained that *Love Hurts* on her 1992 single and album?

1 Can you remember who reached No 1 in 1956 with *I Forgot To Remember To Forget*?

2 Who has recorded under the pseudonym of Buster Poindexter?

3 Described as the 'first post-punk band' which band's name is often shortened to PiL?

4 Brothers Ray and Dave Davies together constituted one half of which famous British band?

5 Which American band were notorious for their weird face paint and costumes? One of their later albums was the 1998 *Psycho Circus*.

6 The song *Leader Of The Pack* was a No 1 hit single in 1964 for which girl band?

7 Which song from Lou Reed's album *Transformer*, released as a single in 1972, is generally regarded as his best and most famous song?

8 Who first recorded the song *Cry* in 1951, a No 1 hit at the time, and later a hit for Lynn Anderson in 1972, and Crystal Gayle in 1986?

9 What title is common to a song made famous by Gene Pitney and a John Ford-directed western movie of 1962?

10 Who made her American chart debut in 1988 with the song *I Should Be So Lucky*?

11 *Girls Just Want To Have Fun* was a No 1 hit single for which singer in 1983?

12 *America: What Time Is Love?* was a big success in America for which British acid house band in 1991?

13 Which song by Ben E King peaked at No 4 in 1961 and No 9 on its rerelease in 1986?

14 Which former 'Second Lady of the US' co-founded the Parents Music Resource Center?

15 The 1972 Simon and Garfunkel appearance at Madison Square Gardens was in a benefit concert in support of which Democratic presidential candidate?

16 What was Janet Jackson's first Billboard Hot 100 No 1 single?

1   *This Old Heart Of Mine,* a big hit for The Isley Brothers in 1966, was originally intended for recording by which other Tamla band?

2   Whose *See You Later, Alligator* reached the American Top Ten in 1956?

3   *Blueberry Hill* and *Ain't That A Shame* were hits in the 1950s for which musician?

4   What was the song by Barbra Streisand and Neil Diamond that made No 1 in 1978?

5   *Hit The Road Jack* reached the top of the Billboard Hot 100 in 1961. Who sang it?

6   What common title links an album by Bruce Springsteen, a song by Dire Straits and a 1958 movie starring Doris Day?

7   With English lyrics put to a Russian folk tune, which song by Mary Hopkin reached No 2 in America in 1968?

8   Which Puerto Rico-born blind singer/guitarist recorded a highly successful 1969 cover of The Doors' *Light My Fire*?

9 What was the childhood disease that afflicted and threatened to cripple Joni Mitchell in her ninth year?

10 Trent Reznor is the one-man constituent of which music act?

11 Which Pearl Jam single was originally a fan club-only release in 1998, but by popular demand was put on general release the following year?

12 What was the title of Roger Miller's 'travelling hobo' song which reached No 1 in 1965?

13 Which female rocker played the part of Leather Tuscadero in the TV series *Happy Days*?

14 Which controversial American thrash metal band released their album *Christ Illusion* in 2006?

15 In which movie does Prince play the part of The Kid?

16 k.d. lang sang the entire music soundtrack on which 1994 movie starring Uma Thurman?

1 Axl Rose and Izzy Stradlin formed which band in 1985?

2 Which band had the original name of The Outcasts before adopting the name of the town where the band's leader had grown up?

3 Who was born Eileen Regina Edwards, changing to her well-known stage name at an early age?

4 Which band, famous for their cover of *Can't Help Falling In Love,* took its name from the reference number of the British unemployment form?

5 Who wrote and recorded the original version of *I Put A Spell On You* in 1956?

6 What was the title of Carl Douglas' only No 1 hit single – a martial arts-themed song of 1974?

7 Whose band, Blues Inc, created a revival of blues music in America and Europe during the 1960s?

8 *Run It*, taken from his debut album, was a No 1 single in 2006 for which singer?

9 Which band's *Ghost In The Machine* was a major hit single in 1981?

10 Which song by Prince relates to the 'artists neighborhood' of his home town of Minneapolis?

11 Barry McGuire, Kenny Rogers and Gene Clark are just some of the artists whose early experience was gained from within which folk-based group of singers?

12 Jeff Kasenetz and Jeff Katz are considered to be the inventors of which pop music genre term, exemplified by bands such as The Archies?

13 NRBQ is the contracted title of which band, whose eclectic mix of many styles of popular music has resulted in a dedicated cult following?

14 Which American boy-band had most of their early success in Europe – their first single *We've Got It Goin' On* being a big hit there in 1995 but only reaching No 69 in the US?

15 What was the nationality of pop artist Falco?

16 ELO is the contracted title of which British band?

1 Who wrote most of, and performed all of, the music on the soundtrack of the movie *The Killing Fields*?

2 Which musician founded the band Blood Sweat and Tears?

3 *Glad All Over, Bits And Pieces* and *Over And Over* were all big US hits for which 1960s British band?

4 The bands Funkadelic and Parliament were masterminded by which funk/soul/R&B artist?

5 The album *Honky Tonk Angels* featured which trio of country gals?

6 Although he is famous for his hard-hitting topical material, eg *Talking Watergate, Last Thing On My Mind* is possibly the best-known song of which artist.

7 In 1970, *Band Of Gold* was the greatest hit single of which singer?

8 What is the stage name of Karen Michelle Johnston, whose activism has translated into works such as *Short Sharp Shocked*?

9 *Greatest Hitz* is the 2005 'best of' album by which band?

10 What is the nationality of the band Men at Work?

11 *Under A Hoodoo Moon* is the autobiography of which blues/R&B artist, born Malcolm J Rebennack in 1940?

12 What was the title of the 1971 album by Humble Pie recorded live at East Village, New York?

13 What two-word term relates to a Joe Cocker song and a title by which singer Rita Coolidge is known?

14 *Man Enough To Be A Woman* is the autobiography of which artist, who was known as Wayne before he changed his name to Jayne?

15 How tall was R&B singer Little Willie John: 5 feet 4 inches; 6 feet 2 inches or 5 feet nothing?

16 What was the original name of the band which re-formed in 1976 as Dr Buzzard's Original Savannah Band?

1   *You Really Got Me,* a classic song from the 60s by the Kinks, was covered in another famous version by which American band in 1978?

2   *Neither One Of Us (Wants To Be The First To Say Goodbye)* was a 1973 chart-topper for which singer and band?

3   Which country singer married actress Julia Roberts in 1993, the two divorcing in 1995?

4   Who won the 1994 Grammy Award For Best Contemporary Folk Album with *Other Voices, Other Rooms*?

5   A No 1 hit in America in 1967, who recorded the title song to the movie *To Sir With Love*? She married Bee Gee Maurice Gibb in 1969.

6   Which rapper's roster of recordings includes the albums *Da Crime* Family, *Ghetto D,* and *Ice Cream Man*?

7   *Tie A Yellow Ribbon Round The Ole Oak Tree* and *Knock Three Times* were big hit singles for which 1970s band?

8   Which Seattle band was formed in 1984 by Chris Cornell and Hiro Yamamoto?

9 What title is common to a 1971 album by Weather Report and a short story by Ray Bradbury?

10 In which song does Tammy Wynette disclose that "Sometimes it's hard to be a woman"?

11 In 1977, which influential punk band was formed by Exene Cervenka and John Doe in Los Angeles?

12 What links the London address of Sherlock Holmes and the title of a smash hit for Gerry Rafferty in 1978?

13 Whose first (1992) compilation album was entitled *Greatest Misses*?

14 Who released two compilation albums in 1996 – one called *Hits* the other called *Misses*?

15 *Up Up And Away* and *Aquarius/Let The Sunshine In* were two of the most successful singles of which 1960s band?

16 Which 1960 Bobby Darin hit song was derived from *La Mer,* written by Frenchman, Charles Trenet in 1943?

1 Whose song *Steve McQueen* won the 2002 Grammy Award for Best Rock Female Vocalist?

2 Margo Timmins is the vocalist with which Canadian band which specializes in its own style of country and rock music?

3 Which band released a 'best of' compilation double album *Gold* in 2005?

4 Which member of the Beach Boys was engaged in a five-year battle with the draft board from 1967?

5 *Walk Don't Run* is a timeless classic originally released in 1960 by which instrumental band?

6 The Village People comprised 'the native American', 'the construction worker', 'the guy in leather', 'the military man', 'the police officer' and which other?

7 In 1962 the babysitter for Carole King and Gerry Goffin was favored to record a song they had just written. Who was that babysitter and what was the song?

8 Who is the singer/songwriter son of John Lennon, for whom Paul McCartney wrote *Hey Jude*?

9 Coolio's worldwide hit rap song *Gangsta's Paradise* was a rearrangement of whose *Pastime Paradise* of 1976?

10 The song *Turn, Turn, Turn*, written and first recorded by Pete Seeger and later covered by The Byrds, has lyrics taken from which work of literature?

11 In June 1970, which rock band was the first ever to perform at the New York Metropolitan Opera House?

12 In 2002, *Sea Change* became the first album by which singer to enter the Top Ten?

13 Formed in 1967, which five-man line-up had a hit with their first album, *Music From Big Pink*?

14 The band America was formed in which country?

15 Which member of Crosby, Stills, Nash and Young was previously with The Hollies?

16 Who was the lead singer and co-founder of the band Hole?

1   Lauren Hill, Wyclef Jean and Pras Michel were all members of which band?

2   Can, Faust and Tangerine Dream were all bands originating from which country?

3   Johnette Napolitano is the vocalist with which Los Angeles band?

4   What was John Lennon's last No 1 single to be released before he died in 1980?

5   What does BRC, an organization for the promotion and protection of black musicians and artists interests, stand for?

6   Rapper/actress Dana Elaine Owens is better known by which stage name?

7   Which highly controversial Los Angeles band released their live album *Omaha To Osaka* in 1998?

8   What is the full name of Monica, the singer who scored great successes with the singles *The Boy Is Mine* and *Angel Of Mine*?

9   *Mama Told Me Not To Come* is possibly the best-known single of which band which formed in 1968?

10   Who was the British member of the Monkees?

11   Who was the former frontman of Genesis who went solo in 1977 with his single *Solsbury Hill*?

12   Writer of the blues classic *Smokestack Lightning*, what was the stage name of Chester Arthur Burnett?

13   Which band was tagged to Marilyn Manson's name on formation in 1989?

14   The 1983 album *The Final Cut* was the last album of which band in its original form?

15   In 1988, which Spanish singer did Stevie Wonder duet with on the single *My Love*?

16   *Dig!* is a 2004 documentary movie based on the careers of the Dandy Warhols and which other band?

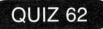

1 What was the title of Bob Dylan's 1962 debut album?

2 For which glam rock band was Johnny Thunders the lead guitarist?

3 *Axel F* by Harold Faltermeyer was the theme tune for which movie starring Eddie Murphy?

4 *Love Train,* of 1973, was a No 1 single for which band?

5 *Wowee Zowee* was the title of which band's third studio album?

6 Known as the Dirt Band in its later years, by what name was this band previously known?

7 The 1997 album *Time And Love* is an all-female compilation album dedicated to which singer who died in that year, aged 49?

8 The Traveling Wilburys was a 'supergroup' comprising George Harrison, Bob Dylan, Tom Petty, Jeff Lynne and which other member?

9 Jimi Hendrix headlined the famous 1969 Woodstock Festival, but at which 1967 music festival did he first achieve fame in America?

10 Whose song, *Mercedes Benz,* written as a comment on materialism, was ironically later used by the car company to advertise their wares?

11 Which singer/instrumentalist took the place of Brian Wilson during the latter's absence from The Beach Boys in 1964/65?

12 At what age did the deaths of Brian Jones, Jimi Hendrix, Janis Joplin, Jim Morrison and Kurt Cobain all occur?

13 Which long-running band's American chart successes have included the albums *Aqualung, Thick As A Brick, Living In The Past* and *War Child*?

14 *One Hell Of A Ride* is a four disk, retrospective album of the work of which country singer?

15 Which band's debut album *Hybrid Theory* propelled them to huge, instant success in 2000?

16 Whose 1974 *Heart Like A Wheel* was (to date) the first of five No 1 albums?

1   *Caravanserai*, an album from 1972, marked a major change of musical direction by which band?

2   What title is common to a 1996 single by the British band The Prodigy and a 1980 novel by Stephen King?

3   What color is common to two 1966 US Top Ten singles – one by The Rolling Stones and one by Los Bravos?

4   Amanda Palmer and Brian Viglione are the two halves of which Boston duo who released two complementary albums, *Yes Virginia* and *No Virginia,* in 2006 and 2008 respectively?

5   Which world-famous band got its biggest break when it won the 1974 Eurovision Song Contest, with the song *Waterloo*?

6   What was Roy Orbison's first US Hot 100 No 1 hit single?

7   *Do Wah Diddy Diddy* was the strange title of the one and only American No 1 hit single by which band?

8   What is the title of the controversial rap single, released in 2005, by Immortal Technique and DJ Green Lantern?

9 What was the title of Eminem's debut album, released in 1999?

10 What title is common to a Bob Dylan No 1 album of 1976 and a 2002 Bryan Adams song?

11 *Allman And Woman: Two The Hard Way* was a 1977 collaboration album by which two artists?

12 What is the title of Norman Greenbaum's famous smash hit of 1970, which propelled him into the charts in many countries?

13 Which album by Madonna was her first to reach the No 1 position in America?

14 Although not very well known outside their native California, the band Oingo Boingo produced one very prolific writer of movie and TV music – including the theme for *The Simpsons*. Who is he?

15 Whose 1999 album, *Echo*, which reached No 10 in the US chart, marked a change in his style?

16 Which Australian duo had two American No 1 hits in the 1990s with *Truly Madly Deeply* and *I Knew I Loved You*?

1 Holding Back The Years (1986) and If You Don't Know Me By Now (1989) are the two American No 1 hit singles by which band?

2 Which novel band with a novel name is probably best remembered for its hit single The Future's So Bright, I Gotta Wear Shades?

3 Which member of Wu-Tang Clan appears on Mary J Blige's I'll Be Here For You/You're All I Need To Get By?

4 The debut album, Shake Your Money Maker (1990) is, to date, the biggest-selling album for which band?

5 Which long-running band's two constant members are the sisters Ann and Nancy Wilson?

6 Layne Staley, Jerry Cantrell, Mike Starr and Sean Kinney were the original members of which band, formed in 1987?

7 Which surf music duo only had one No 1 hit single – Surf City, in 1963?

8 Which singer's short career is marked by the No 1 hits Could've Been and I Think We're Alone Now, taken from her No 1 debut album, released in 1987?

9 Who is the famous singer cousin (born 1940) of Whitney Houston?

10 Which Buddy Holly single was the first to be released after his death, reaching No 1 in the UK but only No 13 in America?

11 Johnny Cash, Willie Nelson, Waylon Jennings and Kris Kristofferson collectively made up which country music supergroup?

12 *Calling Elvis* and *Heavy Fuel* were hit singles (No 3 and No 1 respectively) for which band in 1991?

13 *When I Need You, You Make Me Feel Like Dancing* and *More Than I Can Say* were all big US hits for which British singer?

14 Which band's *Black Holes And Revelations* peaked at No 9 in America in 2006?

15 What was the amazing feat achieved by the band Def Leppard on October 23rd 1995?

16 For which company was Michael Jackson making a commercial when his hair caught fire, in 1984?

1 Which 'protest' song was written and originally recorded by Buffy Sainte-Marie in 1964, and later covered by Donovan and Glen Campbell?

2 *Kiss Me,* sung by Bobby McFerrin, was the theme to which long-running popular TV show during its first three seasons?

3 With which other pop icon does Michael Jackson sing *The Girl Is Mine* on his *Thriller* album?

4 Which classic album provided the hit singles *Mrs Robinson, At The Zoo, Fakin' It* and *Hazy Shade Of Winter*?

5 *The End Of The World* (1963) was the only No 1 single for which singer?

6 Several members of which backing band died with Otis Redding in the plane crash in 1967?

7 *Shelter Me* from the album *Heartbreak Station* was the highest-charting single for which Philadelphia hard rock band?

8 On which album can you hear Brian Wilson's dogs barking against the background noise of a passing locomotive?

9 How did Christine Perfect of the British band Chicken Shack become better known with both a name change and band change in 1969?

10 *Dig Your Own Hole, We Are The Night* and *Exit Planet Dust* are albums by which music duo?

11 In 1991, Aerosmith achieved a first Grammy Award win with which song?

12 Which New York thrash metal band was formed by Scott Ian and Dan Lilker in 1981?

13 What title is common to a 1972 song, from the album *Obscured By Clouds,* by Pink Floyd and a science fiction novel by Arthur C Clarke?

14 On which 2004 song from the album *Confessions,* do Usher and Alicia Keys duet?

15 *The Heart Of Saturday Night* is the second of which artist's albums?

16 The Rossington-Collins Band was originally formed by four of the five surviving members of which band, tragically involved in an airplane crash in 1977?

1 The Quarrymen was a previous name of which famous band?

2 Which famous album, released in 1972, came wrapped in a pair of girls' disposable panties?

3 Which band's single *Sex And Candy* spent a record fifteen weeks at No 1 on the Billboard Modern Rocks chart in 1997-98?

4 Released in 1996, which Nirvana album was a compilation of live performances recorded from 1989 to 1994?

5 *Siamese Dream* is the second studio album of which Chicago band?

6 *Have I Told You Lately,* a big hit for Rod Stewart in 1993, was written and originally recorded by which artist?

7 What title is common to Curtis Mayfield's final album, the fourth album by Poor Righteous Teachers, and a novel by H G Wells?

8 Who, on his 1995 album, *Circus*, announced that *Rock And Roll Is Dead*?

9 Which rapper, to symbolize his change of musical direction, had his dreadlocks cut off during a publicity stunt in 2005?

10 Music producer Tommy Mottola married which singer in 1993?

11 How old was Shakira when she recorded her first album, *Magia*, in 1991?

12 Which band released its fifth compilation album, *Sail On: The 30th Anniversary Collection,* in 2004?

13 *Rebel Yell* (1983), *Whiplash Smile* (1986) and *Charmed Life* (1990), are all albums by which rock star?

14 What did The Ghetto Boys become in 1990?

15 Which New York singing band have released albums featuring the songs of The Grateful Dead, Frank Zappa, The Beatles and U2?

16 *Don't Worry About Me* (released 2002) is a posthumous compilation of the solo songs of which famous band member?

1   *Paul's Boutique,* of 1989, was the second album to be released by which band?

2   What was the title of Blondie's first American No 1 single?

3   Which duo, formed of two singers both named Chris, wore their clothes backwards? Their most famous record was the single *Jump* from 1992.

4   U2's *Hold Me, Thrill Me, Kiss Me, Kill Me* is a 1995 single that appeared on which movie soundtrack?

5   In 1982, which R&B artist was paralyzed after his car crashed through a central divide and hit a tree? He and Whitney Houston duetted on the 1984 hit *Hold Me.*

6   Which founding father of rock 'n' roll, whose innovative guitar effects inspired legions of other musicians, died aged 79 on June 2nd, 2008?

7   Who recorded *Jimmy Mack,* a big hit on both sides of the Atlantic in 1967?

8   Which 1972 hit by the Supremes was later covered by Bananarama?

9 *What's The Frequency Kenneth?* is the enigmatic title of which band's 1994 hit single?

10 *Owner Of A Lonely Heart,* from the 1983 album *90125,* was a No 1 hit for which rock band?

11 Who first recorded *From A Distance*, a song that gave Bette Midler a worldwide hit and several awards for her version of 1990?

12 Which folk singer first visited *Alice's Restaurant* in 1967 and again in 1997?

13 Isaac Hayes appeared in which Mel Brookes-directed 1993 Robin Hood spoof movie?

14 Which alternative country band recorded the Gram Parsons tribute album *Return Of The Grievous Angel*?

15 Lil Wayne's 2008 hit, *Lollipop,* featured which rap performer who died suddenly in February of the same year?

16 What title is common to a Doors song of 1967, the penultimate song on The Beatles' *Abbey Road* album, and a song by Simple Plan on their eponymous album of 2008?

1   Antoine.

2   The Platters.

3   Eddie Cochran.

4   Gene Vincent.

5   The Crazy World of Arthur Brown.

6   Leona Lewis.

7   Phil Spector.

8   *The Bodyguard.*

9   Boyz II Men.

10   Glen Campbell.

11   Brian Wilson.

12   *Don't Cha.*

13   Led Zeppelin.

14   Metallica.

15   Dean Martin.

16   Kurt Cobain.

1 Louis Jordan.

2 *Shake, Rattle and Roll.*

3 Sun Studio.

4 *Sunday Girl* by Blondie.

5 Foo Fighters.

6 Sting.

7 Shea Stadium.

8 The Vandellas.

9 *Top Gun.*

10 Accidental suicide while playing Russian roulette.

11 *Ray.*

12 *The Sound of Music.*

13 Ella Fitzgerald.

14 Dusty Springfield.

15 Australian.

16 Garth Brooks.

1   Kathryn Dawn.

2   Ahmet Ertegun.

3   *Billboard.*

4   Saxophone.

5   Over his use of electric, as opposed to acoustic, instruments.

6   Little Eva.

7   The Asian tsunami disaster of December 26th 2004.

8   Linda Ronstadt.

9   TLC.

10   Tom Jones.

11   T'Pau.

12   *An Englishman in New York.*

13   *Romeo and Juliet.*

14   Johnny Cash.

15   Björk.

16   *Bridge Over Troubled Water.*

QUIZ 4 Answers

1 Johnnie Ray.

2 Neil Diamond.

3 Ice T.

4 Lead guitar, rhythm guitar, bass guitar (or sometimes a stringed double bass) and drum kit.

5 Vincent van Gogh.

6 The Rolling Stones.

7 Patsy Cline.

8 Ireland.

9 Punk.

10 *Nevermind* by Nirvana.

11 The Smashing Pumpkins.

12 Blondie.

13 Carly Simon.

14 Moby.

15 The Who.

16 Madonna.

QUIZ 5 Answers

1   *Sgt Pepper's Lonely Hearts Club Band* by The Beatles.

2   The Saddlemen.

3   Reba McEntire.

4   Frank Sinatra.

5   *Streets of Philadelphia.*

6   Alicia Keys.

7   Bo Diddley.

8   Nancy Sinatra.

9   *Buena Vista Social Club.*

10   Alan Freed.

11   Alicia Keys.

12   Fleetwood Mac.

13   Frankie Goes to Hollywood.

14   Jimi Hendrix.

15   Joey Kramer.

16   Joni Mitchell.

1 Acker Bilk.

2 *Swing When You're Winning.*

3 Wyclef Jean.

4 Michael Jackson.

5 Bo Diddley.

6 Bruce Springsteen.

7 Iceland.

8 *Penny Lane.*

9 The Eagles.

10 Elvis Presley.

11 Ice T.

12 *Song of a Preacher Man.*

13 *Blackboard Jungle.*

14 Christina Aguilera.

15 Jennifer Lopez.

16 Creedence Clearwater Revival.

1   1957.

2   Marilyn Manson.

3   Michael Hutchence.

4   Eric Clapton.

5   Ritchie Valens and the Big Bopper.

6   Sony.

7   Billie Holiday.

8   Cher.

9   Joss Stone.

10   *Songs of Mass Destruction.*

11   Bobby Darin.

12   Cliff Richard.

13   Stevie Wonder.

14   Abba.

15   Destiny's Child.

16   Prince.

1   Chuck Berry.

2   *The Jazz Singer*.

3   Deep Purple.

4   Norah Jones.

5   Coldplay.

6   Tchaikovsky (the ballet was *The Nutcracker*).

7   Linda Eastman.

8   The Jackson Five.

9   Mickey Dolenz.

10   Suzanne Vega.

11   Dolly Parton.

12   Iggy Pop.

13   *Smells Like Teen Spirit* by Nirvana.

14   *My Way*.

15   k.d. lang.

16   *Love Me Tender*.

1 *Maybelline.*

2 Pink Floyd.

3 Aerosmith.

4 Led Zeppelin.

5 Van Halen.

6 *The Raven.*

7 *Mystery Train.*

8 *Classical Gas.*

9 *Come on Over* by Shania Twain.

10 *Bittersweet Symphony.*

11 Pat Boone.

12 The Dixie Chicks.

13 Ike Turner.

14 Kris Kristofferson.

15 Slipknot.

16 Red Hot Chilli Peppers.

QUIZ 10 Answers

1 Lake Erie.

2 The Who.

3 *Knocking on Heaven's Door.*

4 *Earth Song.*

5 Honduras.

6 *Yesterday.*

7 James Brown.

8 Janis Joplin.

9 Dinah Washington.

10 Joan Baez.

11 Grateful Dead.

12 Georgia.

13 Ann-Margret.

14 Elton John.

15 Lee Hazlewood.

16 Mary J Blige.

1   James Brown.

2   Iggy Pop.

3   John Lennon.

4   Tracey Ullman.

5   Gene Pitney.

6   The Four Seasons.

7   Jerry Lee Lewis.

8   Tiny Tim.

9   They all died on stage.

10   Bob Dylan.

11   Johnny Cash.

12   Motown Records.

13   The Jitterbug.

14   Newport, Rhode Island.

15   New York (the song was *Fairytale of New York*).

16   Jim Morrison.

1   Richard Wayne Penniman.

2   *Peter Pan* by J M Barrie.

3   Art Garfunkel.

4   Eminem.

5   Britney Spears.

6   The Ramones.

7   Robinson.

8   Rolling Stone.

9   Queen.

10   Leonard Cohen.

11   Jimmy Preston and his Prestonians.

12   Madonna.

13   Mötley Crüe.

14   Foo Fighters.

15   Curtis Mayfield.

16   Piano Red.

QUIZ 13 Answers

1   Margaret.

2   Frankie Lymon and the Teenagers.

3   U2.

4   Barry McGuire.

5   The Primettes.

6   Roberta Flack.

7   Colonel Tom Parker.

8   Memphis.

9   Scissor Sisters.

10   Diana Krall.

11   Mary J Blige.

12   Perry Como.

13   *Telstar* (the first American No 1 single by any British band).

14   Justin Timberlake.

15   Carole King and Gerry Goffin.

16   The Twist.

1   David Geffen.

2   The Drifters.

3   1955.

4   Donna Summer.

5   Limp Bizkit.

6   Celine Dion.

7   George Harrison.

8   1958.

9   Gloria Estefan.

10 Lionel Richie.

11 The Moody Blues.

12 Roy Orbison.

13 Isaac Hayes.

14 *Titanic*.

15 Germany.

16 Jerry Lee Lewis.

155

1 To attend Bible college.

2 They have all performed the title song to James Bond movies.

3 Vanilla Ice.

4 Aretha Franklin and George Michael.

5 Tamla Motown.

6 The Weather Girls.

7 USA for Africa.

8 Amy Winehouse.

9 Eleven.

10 John Mayer.

11 Village People.

12 Janet Jackson.

13 Eddie Cochran.

14 Johnny Mathis.

15 Germany.

16 Electric guitar.

1   *M.A.S.H.*

2   *Bat Out of Hell.*

3   Bobby McFerrin.

4   Bob Marley and the Wailers.

5   Alice Cooper.

6   Dionne Warwick.

7   REM.

8   Duran Duran.

9   *Enola Gay.*

10   *Do the Bartman.*

11   Missy Elliott.

12   The First Edition.

13   Colombia.

14   The Rolling Stones.

15   Diana Ross.

16   Michael Jackson.

1   Moby.

2   *An Officer And A Gentleman*.

3   Ozzy Osbourne.

4   Jamiroquai.

5   Tupac Shakur.

6   *I am a Rock*.

7   Bobby Brown.

8   Boxcar Willie.

9   Pigmeat Markham.

10   Sheryl Crow.

11   Seattle.

12   1973.

13   Keith Moon of The Who.

14   The Mamas and the Papas.

15   New Zealand.

16   *Midnight Cowboy*.

QUIZ 18 Answers

1   Bruce Springsteen.

2   Kris Kristofferson.

3   *Good Vibrations.*

4   Sophie Ellis-Bextor.

5   Rihanna.

6   Bruce Hornsby.

7   Meatloaf.

8   Debbie Harry.

9   Muscle Shoals.

10   Pearl Jam.

11   Typewriter correction fluid.

12   Lady Lynda.

13   Transcendental Meditation.

14   The Pretenders.

15   Megadeth.

16   *Lola.*

QUIZ 19 Answers

1 The B52s.

2 Bread.

3 Earth, Wind and Fire.

4 Frank Zappa.

5 New Kids on the Block.

6 Steppenwolf.

7 Florence Ballard.

8 *Private Dancer.*

9 1958.

10 The Bangles.

11 Heavy metal.

12 *Things Have Changed.*

13 Annie Lennox.

14 *My Ding-a-Ling.*

15 *Last Thing On My Mind.*

16 Crosby, Stills, Nash and Young.

1   David Bowie.

2   Janet Jackson.

3   *I Will Survive*.

4   The Jackson Five.

5   *Mr Tambourine Man*.

6   Montgomery, Alabama.

7   The Who.

8   *It Takes Two*.

9   Suzanne Vega.

10   Lenny Kravitz.

11   Nina Simone.

12   Jeff Buckley.

13   *Pet Sounds*.

14   Coldplay.

15   Counting Crows.

16   Eva Cassidy.

1   Steve Tyler.

2   Courtney Love.

3   Supertramp.

4   Dolly Parton.

5   Radiohead.

6   Black Eyed Peas.

7   Del Shannon.

8   Manic Street Preachers.

9   *Somethin' Stupid* (originally by Frank and Nancy Sinatra).

10 *Oops! ... I Did It Again.*

11 World Of Music, Arts And Dance.

12 T Rex.

13 Joni Mitchell.

14 Bobby Vee.

15 The Byrds.

16 *Square Pegs*.

1   The Drifters.

2   Moby.

3   Queens Of The Stone Age.

4   *Wipe Out.*

5   To attend the Woodstock Festival.

6   Lilith Fair.

7   *No 1 Record.*

8   Dire Straits.

9   Destiny's Child.

10   *American Pie.*

11   *Supernatural.*

12   *Abbey Road.*

13   *The Dark Side Of The Moon.*

14   *Thriller* by Michael Jackson.

15   Alanis Morissette.

16   Young.

1   Billy Joel.

2   *Meteora.*

3   Victoria Adams.

4   *Tequila.*

5   Ricky Martin.

6   Garth Brooks.

7   Barbra Streisand.

8   Tina Turner.

9   Frank Lloyd Wright.

10   Goldfrapp.

11   Outkast.

12   Louis Armstrong.

13   Sticky Fingaz.

14   Martin Scorsese.

15   Fleetwood Mac.

16   New Order.

1   *People Are Strange.*

2   Tom Jones.

3   2,800 acres.

4   New Kids On The Block.

5   *Private Dancer.*

6   *Saturday Night Fever.*

7   Creedence Clearwater Revival.

8   G Funk/Gangsta Funk.

9   Sonny Bono.

10   Ja Rule.

11   Hilliard.

12   John Lee Hooker.

13   Bobby Brown.

14   Because he had defiled a national monument (The Alamo).

15   Stevie Nicks.

16   The White Stripes.

1   Little Miss Dynamite.

2   Colonel Tom Parker.

3   Carl Perkins.

4   *Hotel California* by The Eagles.

5   *What's The Story (Morning Glory)*.

6   Frank Zappa.

7   The Olympic Games.

8   Justin Timberlake.

9   Jefferson Airplane.

10 Jennifer Lopez.

11 *Thriller*.

12 Amy Winehouse.

13 Jon Bon Jovi.

14 The Miracles.

15 Mariah Carey.

16 *Axel F.*

1   *Tha Doggfather.*

2   Rage Against The Machine.

3   Huey Lewis And The News.

4   Sony.

5   Swedish.

6   *Addicted To Love.*

7   *Please Mr Postman.*

8   1990.

9   Flea.

10   *Mack The Knife.*

11   T-Pain.

12   *Smooth.*

13   *I Got You Babe* by Sonny and Cher.

14   Donovan.

15   P Diddy.

16   *Walk Like An Egyptian.*

1 *Where Is The Love?*

2 *I Will Always Love You.*

3 *Break Like The Wind.*

4 Dr Dre.

5 *Bombs Over Baghdad.*

6 The Moonwalk.

7 Jimmy.

8 Bob Dylan.

9 The Everly Brothers.

10 *Like A Rolling Stone by* Bob Dylan.

11 The Rolling Stones *(I Can't Get No) Satisfaction.*

12 Louis Armstrong.

13 Joni Mitchell.

14 *My Way.*

15 Janis Joplin.

16 *The Philosopher's Stone.*

1   Jamie Foxx.

2   Paris Hilton.

3   *Macarena.*

4   Nu metal.

5   Buggles.

6   Alice Cooper.

7   A medieval torture instrument.

8   Jimmy Webb.

9   *Respect.*

10 *A Whiter Shade Of Pale.*

11 Mötley Crüe.

12 Donald.

13 The Go Go's.

14 *You Can't Hurry Love.*

15 *America.*

16 His father, Marvin Sr.

1   Eazy E.

2   Jane.

3   Guns N' Roses.

4   *1999.*

5   ZZ Top.

6   *The College Dropout.*

7   *How To Dismantle An Atomic Bomb.*

8   The Pips.

9   James Brown.

10 Go-Go.

11 *You Don't Know Me.*

12 Steppenwolf.

13 *Boyz n' The Hood.*

14 Nine Inch Nails.

15 *Taking The Long Way.*

16 Santana.

1   Mark David Chapman, after shooting John Lennon.

2   Katy Perry.

3   Alison Krauss.

4   The Doors.

5   Olivia Newton-John.

6   Rihanna.

7   Biggie Smalls.

8   Vincent Price.

9   He noticed a light had been left on.

10   Elton John.

11   Brenda Lee.

12   The Cars.

13   Prince.

14   France.

15   The Righteous Brothers.

16   The Beach Boys.

1   Peter, Paul and Mary.

2   Earth, Wind and Fire.

3   The Pretenders.

4   The Dandy Warhols.

5   Buffy Sainte-Marie.

6   The Lemonheads.

7   Volkswagen.

8   B B King.

9   'Weird Al' Yankovic.

10   Kenny Rogers and Dolly Parton.

11   Franz Ferdinand.

12   Alice In Chains.

13   P J Proby.

14   *The New Mickey Mouse Club.*

15   *Charlie's Angels.*

16   He used to wear a black and yellow hooped sweater which someone said made him look like a bee.

1   William Shatner.

2   Australian (Helen Reddy).

3   Tori Amos.

4   Rod Stewart.

5   The Rolling Stones.

6   Elvis Presley.

7   Bill Withers.

8   *Another Brick In The Wall.*

9   Alice Cooper.

10   Eric Clapton.

11   Belinda Carlisle.

12   Sandy Denny.

13   Kelly Clarkson.

14   Barry White.

15   Electric Six.

16   Madonna.

1   Hip hop.

2   *Yesterday*, written and first recorded by Paul McCartney.

3   Lou Reed.

4   Oasis.

5   *My Name Is.*

6   George Harrison.

7   Jean-Michel Jarre.

8   Donna Summer.

9   9 to 5.

10   *Better Be Good To Me.*

11   Debbie Harry.

12   *Moon River.*

13   Danny Elfman.

14   Suzanne Vega.

15   *Under The Boardwalk.*

16   Wham!

1   Sam Cooke.

2   *Alice's Adventures In Wonderland.*

3   Curtis Mayfield.

4   *Incesticide.*

5   *In Utero.*

6   Iron Maiden.

7   Smoking tobacco.

8   *Music Of The Sun.*

9   *(Sittin' On) The Dock Of The Bay.*

10   Timbaland.

11   Missy Elliot.

12   Ben E King.

13   *Candle In The Wind.*

14   LA Guns.

15   The Manhattans.

16   Aaliyah.

1   *That'll Be The Day.*

2   Backstreet Boys.

3   *Cracked Rear View.*

4   *Saturday Night Fever.*

5   Chaka Khan.

6   Dionne Warwick.

7   *Band On The Run.*

8   The Pixies.

9   Chuck Berry.

10 Crazy Town.

11 Evanescence.

12 Elvis Costello.

13 Sum 41.

14 Philadelphia.

15 Zager and Evans.

16 The Waitresses.

1   *A Twisted Christmas.*

2   The MGs.

3   Sonny and Cher.

4   Natalie Cole.

5   The Clash.

6   Ladies Love Cool James.

7   Nick Drake.

8   DJ Shadow.

9   The longest held vocal single note.

10   Gwen Stefani.

11   Manic Street Preachers.

12   Michael Jackson and Lionel Richie.

13   *MacArthur Park.*

14   *The Boxer.*

15   Keith Moon.

16   The Communards.

1   Patsy Cline.

2   *Give It Away.*

3   He was in prison.

4   Annie Lennox.

5   *Barcelona.*

6   Public Enemy.

7   Spanish.

8   The Polyphonic Spree.

9   Björk.

10   Eagles Of Death Metal.

11   *...That Restricts Me From Being The Master.*

12   Muse.

13   Jewel.

14   Homelessness.

15   John Denver.

16   Bonnie Raitt.

1   *Great Balls Of Fire.*

2   The Turtles.

3   *Gimme Gimme Gimme.*

4   Norway.

5   Genesis.

6   *Bridge Over Troubled Water.*

7   Joe Cocker.

8   Joe South.

9   Kurt Russell.

10 Percy Sledge.

11 *Candle In The Wind.*

12 *Darling Nikki.*

13 Garbage.

14 Propellerheads.

15 Aretha Franklin.

16 New Order.

1   LeAnn Rimes.

2   *Believe.*

3   Presidents Of The United States Of America.

4   *Time.*

5   *Take On Me.*

6   Dixie Chicks.

7   Green Day.

8   *The Simpsons Movie.*

9   Carrie Fisher.

10 Theme From *Shaft.*

11 Roberta Flack.

12 Pope John Paul II.

13 Shakespeare's Sister.

14 Joan Baez.

15 Jennifer Lopez.

16 Luther Vandross.

1 Sparks.

2 *Arnold Layne.*

3 Sha Na Na.

4 Montreux.

5 *Dangerously In Love.*

6 *Sex And The City.*

7 None.

8 *Take My Breath Away.*

9 Donald Fagen.

10 Canadian.

11 Elvis Costello.

12 *The House Of The Rising Sun.*

13 Beyoncé Knowles.

14 *Two Weeks' Notice.*

15 Gene Pitney.

16 *I Want To Hold Your Hand* (1964).

1   *The Long And Winding Road* (1970).

2   Concert For Bangladesh.

3   They were all songs produced by Phil Spector.

4   The Police.

5   *Hey Hey My My (Into The Black)*.

6   Big Country.

7   The Furious Five.

8   Soul II Soul.

9   Jay Z.

10   Usher.

11   Chic.

12   Muddy Waters.

13   The Beach Boys and The Mamas & The Papas.

14   Crazy Horse.

15   R.E.M.

16   Huey Lewis And The News.

1 Herman's Hermits.

2 *Lord Of The Rings* by JRR Tolkien.

3 James Taylor.

4 Starbucks.

5 Eric Clapton.

6 *Lovesexy.*

7 Billy Preston.

8 With Attitude.

9 Alanis Morrissette.

10 HMV, though both RCA and Victor have used the 'trademark dog' for a time.

11 David Bowie.

12 New York Dolls.

13 Bananarama.

14 The Brian Jonestown Massacre.

15 Japan.

16 Chrissie Hynde.

1   Lee Marvin.

2   Supertramp.

3   *Physical Graffiti.*

4   Gwen Stefani.

5   The Spice Girls.

6   *Tragic Kingdom.*

7   Foxboro Hot Tubs.

8   Feist.

9   *Exodus.*

10   Lil Wayne.

11   Rick Ross.

12   *The College Dropout.*

13   Lynyrd Skynyrd.

14   *Eight Days A Week.*

15   Gwyneth Paltrow.

16   Sleater Kinney.

1   *FutureSex/Love Sounds.*

2   Beethoven.

3   Marvin Gaye.

4   Primal Scream.

5   Dire Straits.

6   Gloria Estefan.

7   Jan and Dean.

8   *Songs For The Deaf.*

9   *PCD.*

10   Busta Rhymes.

11   Q-Tip.

12   *All I Really Want To Do.*

13   The Walker Brothers.

14   *Bohemian Rhapsody.*

15   *LA Woman.*

16   Johnny Rotten.

QUIZ 45 Answers

1   *Grace.*

2   Bruce Springsteen.

3   *Slippery When Wet.*

4   The Killers.

5   Ireland.

6   *Off The Wall.*

7   *Revolver.*

8   Franz Ferdinand.

9   Jane's Addiction.

10   Carole King.

11   INXS.

12   Stevie Wonder.

13   Sly And The Family Stone.

14   Madonna.

15   *Exile On Main Street.*

16   The Cure.

1   The Monkees.

2   Chubby Checker.

3   U2.

4   Yellow Brick Road (on the album *Goodbye Yellow Brick Road*).

5   *Rumours* by Fleetwood Mac.

6   *1001 Albums You Must Hear Before You Die*.

7   *Rust Never Sleeps*.

8   The Rolling Stones.

9   Moby.

10   The Blue Man Group.

11   Kate Bush.

12   Ireland.

13   *Ben*.

14   Chaka Khan.

15   Jimi Hendrix.

16   Captain Beefheart.

1   Keyboard.

2   Ry Cooder.

3   The Boomtown Rats.

4   Bruce Springsteen.

5   Yes.

6   The Stooges.

7   Vangelis.

8   Jane's Addiction.

9   *Give It Away.*

10   Diana Ross.

11   Etta James.

12   Five.

13   50 Cent.

14   L L Cool J.

15   Megadeth.

16   Trans-Siberian Orchestra.

1   Lil Wayne.

2   Usher, Beyonce and Lil Wayne.

3   Bachman Turner Overdrive.

4   Metallica.

5   *The Spy Who Loved Me.*

6   1958.

7   *I Am Because We Are.*

8   T'Pau.

9   All About Eve.

10   1970.

11   Iceland.

12   Vanilla Ice.

13   Scissor Sisters.

14   Supertramp.

15   Gene Vincent.

16   The Lovin' Spoonful.

1   *A Winter's Tale.*

2   *War Of The Worlds.*

3   Genesis.

4   Bread.

5   Al Kooper.

6   *Sgt Pepper's Lonely Hearts Club Band* by The Beatles.

7   *Pet Sounds* by The Beach Boys.

8   The Knack.

9   Bauhaus.

10   *Up On The Roof.*

11   Burt Bacharach and Hal David.

12   Olivia Newton-John.

13   Them.

14   Smokey Robinson.

15   50 Cent.

16   The first manned moon landing.

1   *No One* by Alicia Keys.

2   *Smooth* by Santana ft Rob Thomas.

3   Damita Jo.

4   Celine Dion.

5   *One Week*.

6   Fine Young Cannibals.

7   'Hurricane' Smith.

8   Mariah Carey.

9   Tommy James and the Shondells.

10   Billy Ocean.

11   Roy Orbison.

12   Dr Hook and the Medicine Show.

13   Paul Simon.

14   Chicago.

15   *Graceland*.

16   The Monkees.

QUIZ 51 Answers

1 *By Way Of The Drum.*

2 Milli Vanilli.

3 Bill Wyman.

4 Natasha Bedingfield.

5 Deee-Lite.

6 Janis Martin.

7 Air Supply.

8 *Don't Let The Sun Go Down On Me.*

9 *You're So Vain.*

10 Cat Stevens.

11 *Waiting For Tonight.*

12 Maurice Gibb.

13 Gloria Estefan.

14 Duane Eddy.

15 Gwen Guthrie.

16 The Fugees.

1 Woody Guthrie.

2 The Allman Brothers.

3 The Band.

4 Barry and Robin.

5 Badfinger.

6 Dido.

7 British.

8 Waylon Jennings.

9 *She's So Unusual.*

10 *Mrs Robinson.*

11 Jeannie C Riley.

12 k.d. lang.

13 George Michael.

14 *ABC.*

15 *Bad Moon Rising.*

16 Steppenwolf.

1   Creedence Clearwater Revival.

2   Tina Turner.

3   The Pointer Sisters.

4   Portishead.

5   The Replacements.

6   All Stars.

7   Indigo Girls.

8   Grace Jones.

9   Georgia.

10   Rage Against The Machine.

11   Twisted Sister.

12   Travis Tritt.

13   Neil Sedaka.

14   Korn.

15   The Verve.

16   Macy Gray.

1   Keith Moon.

2   ZZ Top.

3   INXS.

4   Mike Oldfield.

5   Oasis.

6   *OK Computer.*

7   *The Great Escape.*

8   Diana Ross.

9   Pearl Jam.

10 *Size Isn't Everything.*

11 The B52s.

12 *Forbidden.*

13 Americans.

14 Luther Vandross.

15 Bon Jovi.

16 Cher.

1   Elvis Presley.

2   David Johansen.

3   Public Image Limited.

4   The Kinks.

5   Kiss.

6   The Shangri-Las.

7   *Walk On The Wild Side.*

8   Johnnie Ray.

9   *The Man Who Shot Liberty Valance.*

10   Kylie Minogue.

11   Cyndi Lauper.

12   The KLF.

13   *Stand By Me.*

14   Tipper Gore.

15   George McGovern.

16   *When I Think Of You.*

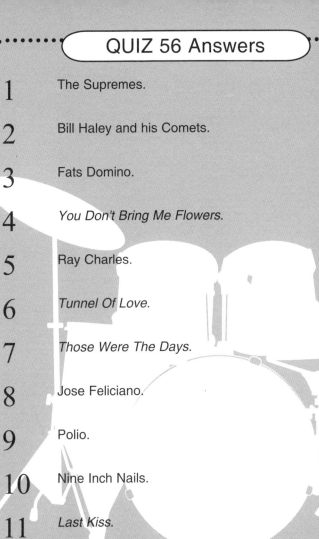

1 The Supremes.

2 Bill Haley and his Comets.

3 Fats Domino.

4 *You Don't Bring Me Flowers.*

5 Ray Charles.

6 *Tunnel Of Love.*

7 *Those Were The Days.*

8 Jose Feliciano.

9 Polio.

10 Nine Inch Nails.

11 *Last Kiss.*

12 *King Of The Road.*

13 Suzi Quatro.

14 Slayer.

15 *Purple Rain.*

16 *Even Cowgirls Get The Blues.*

QUIZ 57 Answers

1   Guns n' Roses.

2   Union Gap.

3   Shania Twain.

4   UB40.

5   Screamin' Jay Hawkins.

6   *Kung Fu Fighting.*

7   Alexis Korner.

8   Chris Brown.

9   The Police.

10   *Uptown.*

11   The New Christy Minstrels.

12   Bubblegum.

13   New Rhythm and Blues Quartet (and earlier, Quintet).

14   Backstreet Boys.

15   Austrian.

16   Electric Light Orchestra.

1   Mike Oldfield.

2   Al Kooper.

3   The Dave Clark Five.

4   George Clinton.

5   Dolly Parton, Loretta Lynn and Tammy Wynette.

6   Tom Paxton.

7   Freda Payne.

8   Michelle Shocked.

9   Limp Bizkit.

10 Australian.

11 Dr John.

12 *Performance Rockin' The Fillmore.*

13 *Delta Lady.*

14 Wayne/Jayne County.

15 Five four.

16 Kid Creole and the Coconuts.

1   Van Halen.

2   Gladys Knight and the Pips.

3   Lyle Lovett.

4   Nanci Griffith.

5   Lulu.

6   Master P.

7   Tony Orlando and Dawn.

8   Soundgarden.

9   *I Sing The Body Electric*.

10   *Stand By Your Man*.

11   X.

12   *Baker Street*.

13   Public Enemy.

14   Joni Mitchell.

15   The Fifth Dimension.

16   *Beyond The Sea*.

1   Sheryl Crow.

2   Cowboy Junkies.

3   The Velvet Underground.

4   Carl Wilson.

5   The Ventures.

6   The 'cowboy'.

7   Eva Boyd – known as Little Eva, who sang *The Loco-Motion*.

8   Julian Lennon.

9   Stevie Wonder.

10   The Bible.

11   The Who (with music from their 'rock opera', *Tommy*).

12   Beck.

13   The Band.

14   Britain.

15   Graham Nash.

16   Courtney Love.

1   The Fugees.

2   Germany.

3   Concrete Blonde.

4   *(Just Like) Starting Over*.

5   Black Rock Coaliton.

6   Queen Latifah.

7   L7.

8   Monica Denise Arnold.

9   Three Dog Night.

10 Davy Jones.

11 Peter Gabriel.

12 Howlin' Wolf.

13 The Spooky Kids.

14 Pink Floyd.

15 Julio Iglesias.

16 The Brian Jonestown Massacre.

1   *Bob Dylan.*

2   New York Dolls.

3   *Beverley Hills Cop.*

4   The O'Jays.

5   Pavement.

6   Nitty Gritty Dirt Band.

7   Laura Nyro.

8   Roy Orbison.

9   Monterey Pop Festival.

10   Janis Joplin.

11   Glen Campbell.

12   27.

13   Jethro Tull.

14   Willie Nelson.

15   Linkin Park.

16   Linda Ronstadt.

1 Santana.

2 *Firestarter.*

3 Black (*Paint It Black* by The Rolling Stones and *Black Is Black* by Los Bravos).

4 The Dresden Dolls.

5 Abba.

6 *Running Scared.*

7 Manfred Mann.

8 *Bin Laden.*

9 *The Slim Shady LP.*

10 *Desire.*

11 Gregg Allman and Cher.

12 *Spirit In The Sky.*

13 *Like A Virgin.*

14 Danny Elfman.

15 Tom Petty.

16 Savage Garden.

1   Simply Red.

2   Timbuk 3.

3   Method Man.

4   The Black Crowes.

5   Heart.

6   Alice In Chains.

7   Jan and Dean.

8   Tiffany.

9   Dionne Warwick.

10   *It Doesn't Matter Any More.*

11   The Highwaymen.

12   Dire Straits.

13   Leo Sayer.

14   Muse.

15   On that day they played concerts on three different continents (in Tangier, London and Vancouver).

16   Pepsi Cola.

1 *Universal Soldier.*

2 The Cosby Show.

3 Paul McCartney.

4 *Bookends* by Simon and Garfunkel.

5 Skeeter Davis.

6 The Bar-Kays.

7 Cinderella.

8 *Pet Sounds* by The Beach Boys.

9 Christine McVie of Fleetwood Mac.

10 The Chemical Brothers.

11 *Janie's Got A Gun.*

12 Anthrax.

13 *Childhood's End.*

14 *My Boo.*

15 Tom Waits.

16 Lynyrd Skynyrd.

1   The Beatles.

2   *School's Out* by Alice Cooper.

3   *Marcy Playground*.

4   *From The Muddy Banks Of The Wishkah*.

5   The Smashing Pumpkins.

6   Van Morrison.

7   *New World Order*.

8   Lenny Kravitz.

9   Busta Rhymes.

10   Mariah Carey.

11   Fourteen.

12   Kansas.

13   Billy Idol.

14   The Geto Boys.

15   The Persuasions.

16   Joey Ramone.

QUIZ 67 Answers

1   Beastie Boys.

2   *Heart Of Glass.*

3   Kriss Kross.

4   *Batman Forever.*

5   Teddy Pendergrass.

6   Bo Diddley.

7   Martha Reeves and the Vandellas.

8   *Nathan Jones.*

9   R.E.M.

10   Yes.

11   Nanci Griffith.

12   Arlo Guthrie.

13   *Robin Hood: Men In Tights.*

14   Whiskeytown.

15   Static Major.

16   *The End.*